D1433409

BRITISH
&
IRISH
ORCHIDS
a field guide

D. M. TURNER ETTLINGER

M

First published 1976 by
THE MACMILLAN PRESS LTD.
London and Basingstoke
Associated companies in
New York, Dublin, Melbourne,
Johannesburg and Madras

ISBN 0 333 18262 6

Filmset and printed by
Thomson Litho Ltd.,
East Kilbride, Scotland

Contents

Preface

There are quite certainly more people—general naturalists, conservationists and country lovers, as well as more serious botanists—who are interested in our native orchids than in any other group of British and Irish wild flowers. Their intrinsic beauty and elaborate life cycle, the difficulty of finding many of the species and the often fine distinctions between them, all offer a series of challenges to an increasing number of people.

There are several good and useful popular flora and guides available, but the trouble with these is that the orchids are only a small proportion of the species covered and there simply is not enough space for more than a superficial treatment of them. The classic *Wild Orchids of Britain* by V. S. Summerhayes is, in fact, the only book available dealing with our orchids alone, and it is not easily used in the field.

This guide does not attempt to supplant Summerhayes' book, which is the product of a lifetime's experience and scholarship, but to supplement it by presenting up-to-date material in a way that can be used readily for search and field identification. Photographic illustrations have been used because they are felt to be more useful than drawings, particularly when the whole plant is shown in its habitat. Short tabulated texts provide other details of each species, and maps show their distribution. Additional chapters are for more leisurely use between excursions.

Just as there are ornithologists and bird-watchers, so there are botanists and plantsmen. This book is unashamedly written for the plantsman, and the minimum possible use has been made of technical terms.

Acknowledgments

I have picked the brains of a legion of orchid-hunting friends and acquaintances in the last few years, and I am grateful to them all. Among individuals, I would particularly acknowledge my debt to C. V. Bulteel, O. Davies, C. R. Nodder, J. H. P. Sankey, P. Went and M. C. F. Proctor.

Many officers of institutions have given considerable help in various ways: the Berks, Bucks and Oxon Naturalists Trust, the Kent Trust for Nature Conservation, the National Museum of Wales, the Nature Conservancy Council and the Royal Botanic Gardens, Kew.

I am grateful to the Botanical Society of the British Isles for permission to derive my distribution maps from their admirable *Atlas of the British Flora,* and to one of the editors, F. H. Perring, for kindly checking that my maps bear a reasonable relationship to the Atlas.

Since my own collection of photographs was not fully comprehensive, some of the illustrations were kindly supplied by the following contributors: A. H. Aston, J. D. Bichard, J. Caldwell, P. Corkhill, S. R. Davey, E. Ferbrache, J. G. Keylock, S. C. Porter, M. C. F. Proctor, G. Rodway, F. Rose and A. Butcher. I am also grateful to the many people who offered photographs which for one reason or another have not been used.

Finally, and with particular warmth, I would acknowledge my considerable debt to two distinguished botanists, R. H. Roberts who has given much expert advice on the difficult genus *Dactylorhiza,* and F. Rose who has advised with equal authority on the other genera.

It is the fate of help and advice that not all of it can always be used, and the above helpers are in no way responsible for the book's remaining shortcomings.

Dorking, 1976   D.M.T.E.

Introduction

There is still a great deal of controversy among experts
about the taxonomic status of some of our orchids; in view
of their variability and their lengthy life cycle (which makes
practical experiments extremely difficult) this is under-
standable. It is particularly marked in the genus *Dactylorhiza*
(Spotted- and Marsh-orchids) where almost any view on
what does or does not constitute a valid species or subspecies can be upheld by one authority or another. In such
a situation, all the non-expert can do is assess the various
arguments and make his own choice; this is the approach
adopted in this book. It should be mentioned that
Sundermann's second edition (p. 141) was published too
recently for notice to be taken of it, even in the 'Other
names' section.

Orchid seeds are so minute that in unstable meteoro-
logical conditions they can be carried great distances by
the wind. The occurrence or maintenance of some of our
rarest species in southeast England is often, and not un-
reasonably, attributed to reinforcement by windborne continental seed. It is therefore rather curious that 'accidentals',
from the large number of non-British continental species,
are not more frequent. The official record only gives one,
the Short-spurred Fragrant Orchid in 1912, and this is
shown briefly here; from time to time one hears rumours
of other continental occurrences, for example Elderflower
Orchid, *Dactylorhiza sambucina*, in Sussex, Woodcock
Orchid, *Ophrys scolopax*, in Kent and Calypso Orchid,
Calypso borealis, in northern Scotland, but as these have not
been authenticated they must be ignored here. Nevertheless,
the possibility of exotic species occurring on an accidental
basis should never be excluded. Though the Channel Islands
are not really British, from a strict biological point of view,
it is a long-standing botanical tradition that they should be
treated as such, and this convention has been followed here.

Scientific names
Given an entity's particular taxonomic status, its scientific
name is governed by a rigorous convention. The names
used here follow J. E. Dandy's *List of British Vascular
Plants* (1958) as modified by his *Nomenclatural Changes in
British Plants* (1969), though one or two of his names in

the genus *Dactylorhiza* are for choices of status not followed here and have been replaced by others.

In the checklist (pp. 11–17), the abbreviation 'ssp' has been used for subspecies (see p. 7) so that their separate authorities can be shown. Elsewhere in the book this abbreviation has been omitted, giving a straight trinomial nomenclature, as has long been customary in ornithology, for example.

English names

In scientific papers, formal lists of records and correspondence with foreigners, the use of scientific names is essential. On other occasions they are usually unnecessary; few British or Irish ornithologists, however expert, would talk to their friends about *Passer domesticus* but would use the vernacular name, House Sparrow.

To be fair, the British Ornithologists' Union has for long had a standard list of vernacular names for British birds, so confusion is most unlikely. Only recently has the Botanical Society of the British Isles followed suit when *English Names of Wild Flowers* by Dony, Perring and Rob was published on the BSBI's behalf in 1974.

Regrettably, there is one BSBI choice, Irish Marsh-orchid, which cannot be followed. This would be fine if one accepted that it was a unique species (*D. kerryensis*) peculiar to Ireland, but the view followed here is that the Irish plant is a subspecies (*occidentalis*) of a widespread European species (*D. majalis*), of which there is another subspecies in Wales (*D. m. cambrensis*). The English name used here for this species, Broad-leaved Marsh-orchid, is not only appropriate to the plant's characteristics but makes a useful pair with the Narrow-leaved Marsh-orchid *D. traunsteineri*.

Incidentally, if *Gymnadenia odoratissima* had been included by the BSBI authors, in order to preserve their binomial policy it would have had to be called Short-spurred Fragrant-orchid, and *G. conopsea* would have had to be altered to Common Fragrant-orchid to be consistent.

The BSBI authors do not venture into subspecific names (it would have been a very difficult task for the entire British flora), but there can be no objection to such things on principle. Some subspecific names are well established (for example, Marsh Fragrant Orchid for *G. conopsea*

2

densiflora) but several have had to be invented. To be logical they have been given trinomial English subspecific names to match their trinomial scientific ones. It is hoped that these names can come into general use.

Other names

While it is not the intention to list every synonym (scientific or English) ever used for a species, the selection chosen here should enable the species to be identified in most older books and lists. In the case of the Broad-leaved Marsh-orchid the BSBI's preference for Irish Marsh-orchid (*D. kerryensis*) is specially noted for those who would like to follow that usage.

Habitat and distribution

Soil type, drainage and degree of shading are important in the occurrence of many of our species. For some, a particular condition or combination may almost constitute a diagnostic difference from other species. For example, a supposed Heath Spotted-orchid found on chalk downland is so improbable that it ought to be examined with extreme care, since it is most probably (though not one hundred per cent certainly) a variant Common Spotted-orchid. But this is not always the case; Greater or Lesser Butterfly-orchids, or both together, are almost equally likely to be found in beechwoods on chalk or in open moorland.

Apart from generalised distribution summaries in the text, the main indication is given in distribution maps for each species. The presentation has been altered from the BSBI Atlas' system of 'occurrence dots' to one of 'probability areas', which are easier to follow, though they may include some ecologically unsuitable territory which should be ignored. 'Habitat' comments should always be borne in mind when studying these maps.

Four categories of probability are shown (the fourth only for rarities):

 Colonies are frequent in suitable habitats: note the word 'suitable' and the comments on downland and marshes on pp. 132–3.

 Colonies are infrequent even in suitable habitats.

 Only very occasional colonies are to be found.

‘Worth keeping an eye open for’, meaning areas where the species has been found in the past, but not recently, where it has been reported but not confirmed, or where it might conceivably extend its range. This is a thoroughly unscientific category and the BSBI are in no way responsible for it.

In accordance with the BSBI's wishes, the more vulnerable rarities' occurrences have been concealed (even further than in the Atlas) by combining the 'very occasional' indication with that for 'worth keeping an eye open for'.

In the author's opinion, it would be quite impracticable for anyone to deduce known rarity sites from these maps or the species pages' comments, or even from the Atlas' originals. It would not be impossible, given enough time and a close scrutiny of maps (see p. 131), but the dedication and time required on the part of the searcher would be prohibitive. If people are determined to find rarity sites, they will do so by other means.

A searcher on the basis of these maps is much more likely to discover previously unknown sites for the rare species, an event which should be welcomed because of the chance that an extra population can be put under the control of some conservation authority and protected against agricultural destruction, forestry, building, and other hazards.

Flowering period

An average range of variation has been built into the dates quoted, but there may be exceptions, due to local conditions or the weather prevailing during the growing season (which, for some species, may include the previous autumn and winter).

A summary chart of all species' flowering dates is included separately on pp. 22–27. This is intended for use when planning excursions or holidays.

Field characters

The chief description of the species lies in the plates: black and white of the whole plant, opposite each species page, and colour of the flower head only, separately. There is no need for a formal botanical description, and technical terms have been used as little as possible when describing differences between species. The bare minimum is illustrated in figure 1.1.

Choice of which points are of special importance is to a large extent personal. Smell, for example, is a most individual matter, and the heavy smoker may well be incapable of recognising even quite strong scents. Differences of spur length and shape (heavily accented in the formal flora) have always seemed to the author difficult to follow; they are mentioned in the text but, unless very marked (for example Fragrant Orchid versus Common Spotted-orchid), not much weight is attached to them.

Photographs have been preferred to drawings because of their greater realism, and the possibility of showing more clearly the habitat (at least in the whole-plant plates). Of course, to get photographs of all species in full flower in exactly typical habitats would have taken more years than the author (and his contributing helpers) have had available. Some shots of flowers in bud or in fruit have been selected because they show the habitat better than other available material. Similarly, some atypical habitats have had to be shown because of the non-availability of better material. British and Irish photographs have been used even when technically better continental shots have been available. For reasons of space, not every possible variation, or even sub-species, is illustrated.

Variation

Many species show much variation between individuals in the same colony, and some (particularly the self-fertile species) vary a good deal between colonies. In the field characters sections, therefore, features often have to be qualified by expressions such as 'usually', 'on average'.

Particularly among the Spotted- and Marsh-orchids, an extreme of variation in one species may overlap an opposite extreme in another. There is also the hazard of hybridisation, so the most one can say about an individual plant in mixed colonies is sometimes that it is probably one species but possibly the other, or possibly a hybrid; exact determination in the field may be impossible. In such circumstances the unit of identification is the colony; if one finds, say, a single plant within the range of variation of the Narrow-leaved

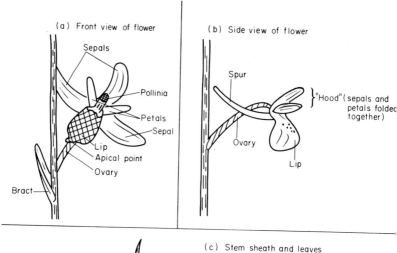

(a) Front view of flower

Sepals

Pollinia

Petals

Sepal

Lip

Apical point

Ovary

Bract

(b) Side view of flower

Spur

"Hood" (sepals and petals folded together)

Ovary

Lip

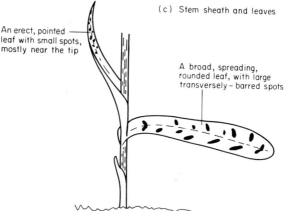

(c) Stem sheath and leaves

An erect, pointed leaf with small spots, mostly near the tip

A broad, spreading, rounded leaf, with large transversely – barred spots

Figure 1.1   Orchid parts useful in flower identification.

Marsh-orchid in a colony of otherwise indubitable Southern Marsh-orchids, the odds would be that the plant is a variant Southern. A proportion of, say, five per cent of such plants, however, might indicate a mixed colony of both species. There are exceptions: the Southern Marsh-orchid itself is liable to turn up singly on chalk downland surrounded by large numbers of Common Spotted-orchids. Similarly, the characteristic sharp folding of the lip in the Early Marsh-orchid is recognisable even in a single specimen, albeit hybridised perhaps, surrounded by other species.

Subspecies and forms

Till quite recently, regular major variations within a plant species were all referred to as *varieties* (abbreviation var., sometimes followed by a distinctive scientific title), without commitment as to whether the variation was random, genetic in origin, or merely the result of habitat conditions.

The subspecies concept, long current in other branches of biology, has now been fairly widely accepted in botany. Since it may be new to some readers, a short explanation seems necessary.

A subspecies can be considered as a regular variation from the type, genetically controlled and allied to some sort of isolation from the rest of the population. The isolation can be geographical, by adaptation to a different type of habitat, or by difference in flowering date, for example. If it could be grown in an ordinary inland marsh, seed from a Dune Early Marsh-orchid (*D. incarnata coccinea*) would, it is presumed, still produce flowers with the characteristics of the Dune subspecies, because those depend now on inheritance only and not on the different habitat which gave an originally random mutation a chance to develop into a population distinct from ordinary Early Marsh-orchids.

Other types of difference from the normal, not genetically controlled, are usually simple responses by the individual plant to its environment, and are referred to here as *forms*. It is presumed that seed from a Greater Butterfly-orchid (woodland form), if grown on a moor, would turn out to be Greater Butterfly-orchids (moorland form). Experiments to verify such presumptions are rarely possible, hence much of the doubt over some entities' exact status. The stage at which differences should be considered specific rather than subspecific is another major source of contention among the experts.

A complication is provided by those species which are self-fertile, for example some *Epipactis* Helleborines, since the different characters of each colony are clearly inherited. But the variation does not seem to be allied to any sort of isolation, so it fails one of the tests of a subspecies. Such variants are also referred to here as forms (f., followed by a distinctive scientific title where one has been given).

Hybrids

Most orchids will readily hybridise within their own genus and occasionally outside it. This is the basis of the commercial orchid industry, in southeast Asia particularly.

In these islands, bigeneric hybrids are unlikely to lead to any serious identification problem; the characters of the genera are so different that a mix will immediately strike the eye as strange, after which it should be a fairly simple matter to isolate the species concerned. They are also rare; among all the thousands of Fragrant Orchids seen by the author growing with Common Spotted-orchids, so far he has found only three hybrids between them!

Hybrids of species within a genus are more frequent but even then (with the exception of the Marsh- and Spotted-orchids) they are far from common. They are perhaps overlooked for it needs a sharp eye to pick up a hybrid White × Narrow-leaved Helleborine or a Greater × Lesser Butterfly-orchid in a large mixed colony.

Hybridisation among the Marsh- and Spotted-orchids (the genus *Dactylorhiza*) is common, however, and a major contributor to the uncertainty of identifying a single variant plant in a mixed colony. Many such hybrids do exhibit hybrid vigour, being larger and more densely flowered than others in the colony; these often stand out but the feature is not universal. A complete intermediate merging of the characters of the parents seems to be uncommon, most hybrids showing individual characters from both parents; for example, a hybrid Early Marsh × Southern Marsh might have the leaves, stem and flower colour of the Southern Marsh and the lip shape and markings of the Early Marsh.

If hybrids were as fertile as their parents, their frequent vigour (which gives them a natural-selection advantage) would soon ensure that they became dominant; sites would be full of that botanist's bogey—the unidentifiable hybrid swarm whose parent species had disappeared. Fortunately, when hybrids set seed its viability is very low; the majority of hybrids end their lives without descendants. A balance with the parent populations is eventually reached, the proportion depending on the strength of the selection pressures which favour the hybrid.

In one mixed colony in normal circumstances, the hybrid population was shown to be not more than four per cent. However, where selection pressures are heavy, for example after a site has been ploughed up, when scrub is invading or when a marsh is partially drained, one can expect the proportion of hybrids to be higher; the total population will be smaller, because of the non-survival of most of the parent species, and will continue to decline because of the hybrids' infertility. It is fair to add that this classical explanation is not always observable in practice.

Checklist of British and Irish orchids

For comments on the selection of entries, and the choice of names (scientific and English) see pp. 1–2.

The genus/species numbers are Dandy's (1958), see p. 1. The serial numbers are for this book only; each species page and plate is marked with this number for ease of cross reference.

Status is assessed on the following basis:

VR	very rare	Fewer than ten known regular colonies
R	rare	Between ten and a hundred known colonies
S	scarce	Very local (though perhaps in large colonies where it does occur), or in very small numbers if widespread
C	common	The sort of plant one could reasonably expect to see in any suitable habitat without a special search
CI	Channel Islands only	
A	accidental	
Ex	extinct	

Hybrids
A full checklist of all recorded hybrids is unnecessary in a book of this sort. Spotted- and Marsh-orchid hybrids, however, are so common that a list is thought to be useful (pp. 18–20).

Serial	Genus/species	English name	Scientific name	Status
1	623/1	Lady's-slipper	*Cypripedium calceolus* L.	VR
2	624/1	White Helleborine	*Cephalanthera damasonium* (Mill.) Druce	S
3	624/2	Narrow-leaved Helleborine	*Cephalanthera longifolia* (L.) Fritsch	R
4	624/3	Red Helleborine	*Cephalanthera rubra* (L.) Rich.	VR
5	625/1	Marsh Helleborine	*Epipactis palustris* (L.) Crantz	S
6	625/2	Broad-leaved Helleborine	*Epipactis helleborine* (L.) Crantz	C
7	625/3	Violet Helleborine	*Epipactis purpurata* G. E. Sm.	R
8	625/4	Narrow-lipped Helleborine	*Epipactis leptochila* Godfery	R
9	625/5	Dune Helleborine	*Epipactis dunensis* (T. & T. A. Stephenson) Godfery	VR
10	625/6	Green-flowered Helleborine	*Epipactis phyllanthes* G.E. Sm.	R
11	625/7	Dark-red Helleborine	*Epipactis atrorubens* (Hoffm.) Schult.	R
12	626/1	Ghost Orchid	*Epipogium aphyllum* G. E. Sm.	VR

Serial	Genus/species	English name	Scientific name	Status
13	627/1	Autumn Lady's-tresses	*Spiranthes spiralis* (L.) Chevall.	S
14	627/2	Summer Lady's-tresses	*Spiranthes aestivalis* (Poir) Rich.	Ex
15	627/3	Irish Lady's-tresses	*Spiranthes romanzoffiana* Cham.	R
16	628/1	Twayblade	*Listera ovata* (L.) R.Br.	C
17	628/2	Lesser Twayblade	*Listera cordata* (L.) R.Br.	R
18	629/1	Bird's-nest Orchid	*Neottia nidus-avis* (L.) Rich.	S
19	630/1	Creeping Lady's-tresses	*Goodyera repens* (L.) R.Br.	S
20	631/1	Bog Orchid	*Hammarbya paludosa* (L.) Kuntze	R
21	632/1	Fen Orchid	*Liparis loeselii* (L.) Rich, ssp *loeselii*	VR
	632/1	Broad-leaved Fen Orchid	*Liparis loeselii* ssp *ovata*, Riddelsd.	R
22	633/1	Coralroot Orchid	*Corallorhiza trifida* Chatel.	R
23	634/1	Musk Orchid	*Herminium monorchis* (L.) R.Br.	S
24	635/1	Frog Orchid	*Coeloglossum viride* (L.) Hartm.	S

Serial	Genus/species	English name	Scientific name	Status
25	636/1	Fragrant Orchid	*Gymnadenia conopsea* (L.) R.Br., ssp *conopsea*	C
	636/1	Marsh Fragrant Orchid	*Gymnadenia conopsea* ssp *densiflora* (Wahlenb.) Camus G. & A., & Berg	S
26	636/2	Short-spurred Fragrant Orchid	*Gymnadenia odoratissima* (L.) Rich.	A
27	637/1	Small-white Orchid	*Pseudorchis albida* (L.) A. & D. Loeve	R
28	638/1	Greater Butterfly-orchid	*Platanthera chlorantha* (Custer) Reichb.	S
29	638/2	Lesser Butterfly-orchid	*Platanthera bifolia* (L.) Reichb.	S
30	639/1	Dense-flowered Orchid	*Neotinea intacta* (Link.) Reichb. f.	R
31	640/1	Bee Orchid	*Ophrys apifera* Huds.	S
32	640/2	Late Spider-orchid	*Ophrys fuciflora* (Crantz) Moench.	VR
33	640/3	Early Spider-orchid	*Ophrys sphegodes* Muell.	R
34	640/4	Fly Orchid	*Ophrys insectifera* L.	S
35	641/1	Lizard Orchid	*Himantoglossum hircinum* (L.) Spreng.	VR

Serial	Genus/species	English name	Scientific name	Status
36	642/1	Lady Orchid	*Orchis purpurea* Huds.	R
37	642/2	Military Orchid	*Orchis militaris* L.	VR
38	642/3	Monkey Orchid	*Orchis simia* Lam.	VR
39	642/4	Burnt Orchid	*Orchis ustulata* L.	R
40	642/5	Green-winged Orchid	*Orchis morio* L.	R
41	642/6	Loose-flowered Orchid	*Orchis laxiflora* Lam.	CI
42	642/7	Early-purple Orchid	*Orchis mascula* L.	C
43	643/1a	Common Spotted-orchid	*Dactylorhiza fuchsii* (Druce) Soó, ssp *fuchsii*	C
	643/1b	Irish Common Spotted-orchid	*Dactylorhiza fuchsii* ssp *okellyi* (Druce) Soó	S
	643/1c	Hebridean Common Spotted-orchid	*Dactylorhiza fuchsii* ssp *hebridensis* (Willmott) Soó	R
44	643/2b	Heath Spotted-orchid	*Dactylorhiza maculata* (L.) Soó ssp *ericetorum* (E. F. Linton) Hunt & Summerh.	C
	643/2a	Rhum Heath Spotted-orchid	*Dactylorhiza maculata* ssp *rhoumensis* (H. Harrison f.) Soó	VR

Serial	Genus/species	English name	Scientific name	Status
45	643/3a	Early Marsh-orchid	*Dactylorhiza incarnata* (L.) Soó ssp *incarnata*	C
	643/3b	Purple Early Marsh-orchid	*Dactylorhiza incarnata* ssp *pulchella*, (H. Harrison f.) Soó	S
	643/3c	Dune Early Marsh-orchid	*Dactylorhiza incarnata* ssp *coccinea* (Pugsl.) Soó	S
	643/3d	Flecked Early Marsh-orchid	*Dactylorhiza incarnata* ssp *cruenta* (Muell.) Sell.	R
	643/3f	Fen Early Marsh-orchid	*Dactylorhiza incarnata* ssp *ochroleuca* (Boll) Hunt & Summerh.	VR
46	643/4	Southern Marsh-orchid	*Dactylorhiza praetermissa* (Druce) Soó	S
47	643/5	Northern Marsh-orchid	*Dactylorhiza purpurella* (T. & T. A. Stephenson) Soó	C
48	Not listed as such	Irish Broad-leaved Marsh-orchid	*Dactylorhiza majalis* (Reichb.) Hunt & Summerh., ssp *occidentalis* (Pugsl.) D. A. Webb	R
	Not listed	Welsh Broad-leaved Marsh-orchid	*Dactylorhiza majalis* ssp *cambrensis* R. H. Roberts	VR

Serial	Genus/species	English name	Scientific name	Status
49	643/7	Narrow-leaved Marsh-orchid	*Dactylorhiza traunsteineri* (Sauter) Soó	R
50	644/1	Man Orchid	*Aceras anthropophorum* (L.) Ait. f.	S
51	645/1	Pyramidal Orchid	*Anacamptis pyramidalis* (L.) Rich.	C

Spotted- and Marsh-orchid hybrids

Abbreviations

CSO	Common Spotted-orchid	**NMO**	Northern Marsh-orchid
HSO	Heath Spotted-orchid	**BLMO**	Broad-leaved Marsh-orchid
EMO	Early Marsh-orchid	**NLMO**	Narrow-leaved Marsh-orchid
SMO	Southern Marsh-orchid		

Common Spotted-orchid	× HSO	*Dactylorhiza × transiens* (Druce) Soó
	EMO	*Dactylorhiza × kernerorum* (Soó) Soó
	SMO	*Dactylorhiza × grandis* (Druce) P. F. Hunt
	NMO	*Dactylorhiza × venusta* (Steph.) Soó
	BLMO	*Dactylorhiza × braunii* (Halaczy) Borsos & Soó
	NLMO	*Dactylorhiza × kellerana* (Ciff. & Giac.) Soó
Heath Spotted-orchid	× CSO	*Dactylorhiza × transiens* (Druce) Soó
	EMO	*Dactylorhiza × claudiopolitana* (Soó) Soó
	SMO	*Dactylorhiza × hallii* (Druce) Soó
	NMO	*Dactylorhiza × formosa* (Steph.) Soó
	BLMO	*Dactylorhiza × townsendiana* (Rouy) Soó
	NLMO	*Dactylorhiza × jenensis* (Brandt) Soó

Early Marsh-orchid	× CSO	*Dactylorhiza* × *kernerorum* (Soó) Soó
	HSO	*Dactylorhiza* × *claudiopolitana* (Soó) Soó
	SMO	*Dactylorhiza* × *wintoni* (Camus)
	NMO	*Dactylorhiza* × *latirella* (Hall) Soó
	BLMO	*Dactylorhiza* × *aschersoniana* (Haussknecht) Soó
	NLMO	*Dactylorhiza* × *lehmanni* (Klinge) Soó
Southern Marsh-orchid	× CSO	*Dactylorhiza* × *grandis* (Druce) P. F. Hunt
	HSO	*Dactylorhiza* × *hallii* (Druce) Soó
	EMO	*Dactylorhiza* × *wintoni* (Camus)
	NMO	*Dactylorhiza* × *insignis* (Brandt) Soó
	BLMO	Not described
	NLMO	Not described
Northern Marsh-orchid	× CSO	*Dactylorhiza* × *venusta* (Steph.) Soó
	HSO	*Dactylorhiza* × *formosa* (Steph.) Soó
	EMO	*Dactylorhiza* × *latirella* (Hall) Soó
	SMO	*Dactylorhiza* × *insignis* (Brandt) Soó

	BLMO	Not described
	NLMO	Not described
Broad-leaved Marsh-orchid	× CSO	*Dactylorhiza × braunii* (Halaczy) Borsos & Soó
	HSO	*Dactylorhiza × townsendiana* (Rouy) Soó
	EMO	*Dactylorhiza × aschersoniana* (Haussknecht) Soó
	SMO	Not described
	NMO	Not described
	NLMO	*Dactylorhiza × dufftiana* (Schulze) Soó
Narrow-leaved Marsh-orchid	× CSO	*Dactylorhiza × kellerana* (Ciff. & Giac.) Soó
	HSO	*Dactylorhiza × jenensis* (Brandt) Soó
	EMO	*Dactylorhiza × lehmanni* (Klinge) Soó
	SMO	Not described
	NMO	Not described
	BLMO	*Dactylorhiza × dufftiana* (Schulze) Soó

It should be noted that these names apply irrespective of the subspecies of the parent plant concerned.

3 Flowering-date chart

No	Species	Apr
1	Lady's-slipper	
2	White Helleborine	
3	Narrow-leaved Helleborine	
4	Red Helleborine	
5	Marsh Helleborine	
6	Broad-leaved Helleborine	
7	Violet Helleborine	
8	Narrow-lipped Helleborine	
9	Dune Helleborine	
10	Green-flowered Helleborine	
11	Dark-red Helleborine	
12	Ghost Orchid	
13	Autumn Lady's-tresses	
15	Irish Lady's-tresses	
16	Twayblade	
17	Lesser Twayblade	
18	Birds-nest Orchid	

...y	June	July	August	September

No	Species	Ap
19	Creeping Lady's-tresses	
20	Bog Orchid	
21	Fen Orchid	
22	Coralroot Orchid	
23	Musk Orchid	
24	Frog Orchid	
25	Fragrant Orchid	
27	Small-white Orchid	
28	Greater Butterfly-orchid	
29	Lesser Butterfly-orchid	
30	Dense-flowered Orchid	
31	Bee Orchid	
32	Late Spider-orchid	
33	Early Spider-orchid	
34	Fly Orchid	
35	Lizard Orchid	
36	Lady Orchid	

May	June	July	August	September

No	Species	Apri
37	Military Orchid	
38	Monkey Orchid	
39	Burnt Orchid	
40	Green-winged Orchid	
41	Loose-flowered Orchid	
42	Early-purple Orchid	
43	Common Spotted-orchid	
44	Heath Spotted-orchid	
45	Early Marsh-orchid	
46	Southern Marsh-orchid	
47	Northern Marsh-orchid	
48	Broad-leaved Marsh-orchid	
49	Narrow-leaved Marsh-orchid	
50	Man Orchid	
51	Pyramidal Orchid	

May	June	July	August	September
	▓			
▓				
▓	▓	▓		
▓				
▓				
▓				
	▓	▓		
	▓	▓		
	▓	▓		
	▓			
	▓	▓		
▓	▓	▓		
▓				
▓				
	▓	▓	▓	

4 Species pages

The details of each species have been tabulated in the following standard way.

Other names
For the principles employed, see p. 3.

Habitat and distribution
The geographical and ecological factors important in the species' occurrence are summarised (see also p. 3).

The distribution maps, based on *The Atlas of the British Flora,* are explained in more detail on pp. 3–4. Some amendments to *Atlas* data have been incorporated in the light of other evidence, and there are a few differences based on differing taxonomic views; these are discussed on pp. 1–2.

The legend, analysed in more detail on pp. 3–4, is reproduced on each page:

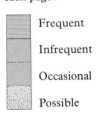

Frequent

Infrequent

Occasional

Possible

Flowering period
An average degree of variation has been built in (see p. 4) and the dates quoted are summarised in the charts on pp. 22–27.

Field characters
The chief description lies in the plates—black and white of the whole plant, opposite each species description (see pp. 4–5), and colour of the flower-heads in chapter 5.

In the text, particular emphasis has been placed on characters which differentiate one species from others with which it is likely to be confused.

Variation
The prevalence of variation, subspecies and forms, and hybrids have been discussed on pp. 5–6; hybrids of Spotted- and Marsh-orchids are listed on pp. 18–20.

1 Lady's-slipper
Cyripedium calceolus

Other names Nil.

× ½ Pennines

Habitat and distribution

In this country it has invariably been found on limestone, and usually on steep hillsides or scree, in open woodland or scrub. Associated trees may be oak, ash, rowan, and/or hazel.

It has been found on north-facing slopes at or above 500 feet (165 m), though occurrence on the flat or at low level is by no means impossible.

The greed of plant collectors has reduced the species to near extinction. One Pennine colony is known and, considering the large tracts of suitable country in the Peak, Dales and Lake districts, overlooked colonies are very possible. A single plant has recently been found in northwest England but its authenticity as a wild (not introduced) specimen is not confirmed.

Individual plants may be long lived but do not necessarily produce flowers every year.

Flowering period

Mid May to early July, mostly mid/late June.

Field characters

Colour plate II(*a*).
Height 6–12 in (15–30 cm).
The flower's colouring, size and shape are quite unmistakable.

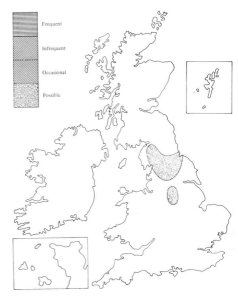

Frequent

Infrequent

Occasional

Possible

Variation

Wild plants vary little.

Attempts to reintroduce cultivated specimens into former wild areas have been made. Some of these might be of related foreign species.

White Helleborine
Cephalanthera damasonium

Other names Large White or Broad Helleborine,
Poached-egg Plant, *Cephalanthera latifolia.*

× ½ Surrey

Habitat and distribution

It occurs almost exclusively on chalk or limestone, usually in shade, sometimes heavy (bare beechwood floors are a favourite type of site). It is also found in wood-edge scrub and occasionally on grassy slopes in the open.

Colonies are often large and frequent within the distribution area which is different from that of the Narrow-leaved Helleborine **3,** though they do overlap in southeast England.

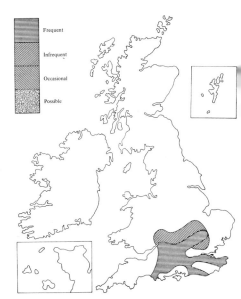

Frequent

Infrequent

Occasional

Possible

Flowering period

Mid May to early July.

Field characters

Colour plate II(*b*).
Height 6–18 in (15–45 cm).
The general appearance is unmistakable except for resemblance to the Narrow-leaved Helleborine **3,** from which it can be distinguished by the following features.

Broad, relatively erect, elliptical leaves.

Flowers also erect and close to the stem.

Bracts longer than the adjacent ovaries.

Flowers a creamier white and less widely opening (indeed most do not really open at all).

Sepals with blunt tips.

Variation

The amount of flower opening depends on local conditions that year. Plants growing in the open are shorter, sturdier and earlier flowering than specimens in heavy shade.

Narrow-leaved Helleborine
Cephalanthera longifolia

Other names Long-leaved, Sword-leaved or Narrow Helleborine, *Cephalanthera ensifolia.*

× ⅔ Hampshire

Habitat and distribution

It is usually found on chalk or limestone, sometimes sandstone, in well-drained situations, and is most frequent in open woods of oak, ash or beech, or in scrub at their edges. It also occurs occasionally (in Ireland) in the open on stabilised dunes.

Distribution is widespread but few suitable sites are occupied; colonies in southeast England may be mixed with White Helleborines **2**. Numbers vary a good deal from year to year.

Flowering period

Mid May to mid June, one to two weeks earlier than the White Helleborine.

Field characters

Colour plate II(*c*).
Height 3–24 in (7–60 cm), usually 9–18 in (23–45 cm).

It differs from the White Helleborine by having the following features.

Leaves relatively long, parallel-sided and thin, horizontal or drooping in general effect.

Bracts shorter than adjacent ovaries.

Flowers spread more horizontally away from the stem.

Sepals pointed at the ends.

Flowers a purer white and wider opening.

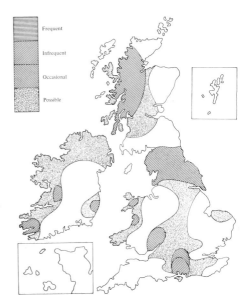

Frequent

Infrequent

Occasional

Possible

Variation

Irish sand-dune specimens may be miniatures only 3 in (7 cm) high.

Hybrids × White Helleborine have occurred in mixed colonies and are recognised by having a mix of the distinguishing features.

4

Red Helleborine
Cephalanthera rubra

Other names Nil.

× ½ Cotswolds (S. C. Porter)

Habitat and distribution

Colonies are invariably on chalk or limestone in hilly country with beechwoods; they are usually on bare floors in these woods (sometimes with a little bramble or dog's mercury) but could be in scrub at their edges.

Individual plants are long lived but have an apparently critical requirement for the balance of light and shade. In unfavourable circumstances a colony may persist for years without a flower being produced; even leafy shoots may be scarce or absent.

It is now an extreme rarity, known only from four or five sites in the Cotswolds and one in the Chilterns. Despite the bright flower colour, colonies may exist which have been overlooked, because of the infrequency of flowering. There have been several recent years when no flower has been recorded in England at all.

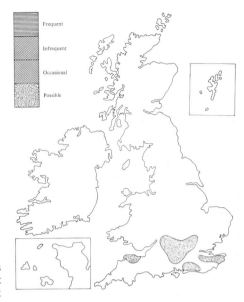

Flowering period

Early June to late July. Seed is rarely set, so when a flower does occur it may be long lasting.

Field characters

Colour plate II(*d*).
Height 12–30 in (30–75 cm), but non-flowering specimens may be much shorter.

Some plants are weedy-looking, tending to fall over under their own weight.

Otherwise the habit is much as the Narrow-leaved Helleborine **3,** but the flowers are a brilliant pink, brighter than the reddest of Broad-leaved or Dark-red Helleborines **6** or **11,** whose flowers and leaves are of a quite different shape, too.

It can still be distinguished from the Narrow-leaved Helleborine even when not flowering by its violet stem sheath (but beware of confusion with non-flowering Broad-leaved or Narrow-lipped Helleborines **6** or **8**).

Variation

Albinos have been recorded on the Continent.

5

Marsh Helleborine
Epipactis palustris

Other names Nil.

× ½ Londonderry

Habitat and distribution

It usually occurs in fens and marshes with alkaline water supplies, and commonly on the slacks in dune systems, but not in sphagnum bogs.

It is fairly widespread in suitable places and colonies may be very large. Occasionally, for example in Kent, Surrey and Wiltshire, it occurs in small numbers on chalk downland, far from water.

Flowering period

Late June to early September, mostly mid July to mid August.

Field characters

Colour plate II(*e*).
Height 6–18 in (15–45 cm).

The brownish and white flowers, with a yellow spot on the frilly white lip, are distinctive.

Variation

Dune-slack specimens are often short and stocky.

f. *ochroleuca* has flowers a yellowish-white overall, and is not uncommon as a component in colonies where the rest of the flowers are normal.

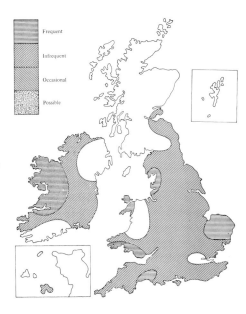

Frequent

Infrequent

Occasional

Possible

6

Broad-leaved Helleborine
Epipactis helleborine

Other names Common or Broad Helleborine, *Epipactis latifolia.*

× ¼ Surrey

Habitat and distribution

It is commonest on chalk or limestone with thin soil cover but occurrence on other soils is quite frequent, preferably in shade (sometimes dense) but also at times in the open. Beech-woods are preferred, usually near the edges or in clearings, but oakwoods, scrub, scree slopes and stabilised dunes can also be used. It can persist or even appear in plantations of alien conifers, at least for a while.

It is a fairly common species, widely distributed, and colonies may be large.

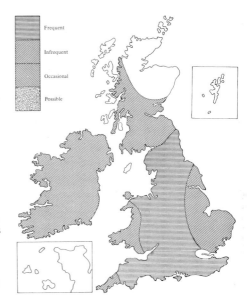

Flowering period

Early July to late August (mostly in early August).

Field characters

Colour plate III(*a*).
Height 4–40 in (10–100 cm).

The leaves are broad and blunt, usually (but not always) in three rows, the lower ones being egg shaped. The colour of leaves and stem varies from pale green to purplish, but they never have the greyish tinge of the Violet Helleborine **7.**

Sepals and petals may be any colour from pale green to a dark reddish shade.

The outer lip is heart shaped, the tip being usually invisible because it is folded underneath.

The ovary is smooth, unlike the Dark-red Helleborine **11.**

Variation

The flower colour and lip shape vary much, independently of each other, between individuals and between colonies.

Plants on marginally suitable soils may be dwarfs.

Hybrids have been recorded × Dark-red Helleborine (*Epipactis* × *schmalhauseri*, K. Richt) and × Violet Helleborine (*Epipactis* × *schulzei*, P. Fourn).

7

Violet Helleborine
Epipactis purpurata

Other names Purple-washed or Clustered Helleborine,
Epipactis violacea or *sessiflora*.

× ¼ Surrey

Habitat and distribution

It usually occurs on well-drained, non-chalky clays or on clay-with-flints over chalk, and occasionally on sandy soil.

Colonies are mainly in heavily shaded beechwoods on bare floors but often near their edges, and occasionally in oakwoods.

Distribution is chiefly in southeast England, but the species is very local and many suitable sites are unoccupied.

Flowering period

Late July to late September.

Field characters

Colour plate III(*b*).
Height 12–36 in (30–90 cm).

Clusters are formed more often than in other species of the genus, but single plants are also frequent.

The leaves are noticeably smaller and narrower than nearly all Broad-leaved Helleborines **6** (never egg shaped) and have a diagnostic purplish-grey tinge, particularly on the undersides and most noticeably before the flowers are out.

The flowers are usually pale green, never as wine-coloured as some Broad-leaved **6** or most Dark-red Helleborines **11.**

The lip and sepals are more pointed than the Broad-leaved and the lip tip is less often folded under.

Variation

In a rare form, the whole plant is suffused with a rose or lilac colour, green chlorophyll being quite lacking (f. *chlorotica*).

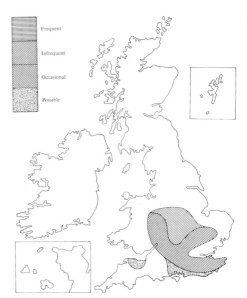

Frequent

Infrequent

Occasional

Possible

43

8

Narrow-lipped Helleborine
Epipactis leptochila

Other names Green-leaved or Slender-lipped Helleborine.

× ⅔ Surrey

Habitat and distribution

It invariably occurs on chalk or limestone with a thin soil-covering, in woods with heavy shade, the usual habitat being a bare-floored beechwood but occasionally oakwood.

Apart from one small colony in Yorkshire, it is only known from southern England. It is possibly still an overlooked species.

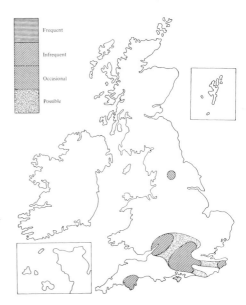

Flowering period

Mid July to early August, slightly earlier than most Broad-leaved Helleborines **6.**

Field characters

Colour plate III(*c*).
Height 6–30 in (15–75 cm).

Many specimens are rather thin and inclined to fall over under their own weight.

Leaves are elliptical rather than oval, narrower than most Broad-leaved Helleborines, and usually in two rows. They are a paler green than other Helleborines, most noticeably before the flowers are out. This may be very obvious.

The flowers are a yellowish- or whitish-green, never reddish.

The lip is long and pointed, not folded underneath.

Variation

This is a self-fertile species, with a good deal of variation between colonies.

f. *cleistogama* (described from Gloucestershire) has flowers which never open properly, but the leaf details distinguish it from similar flowers of the Green-flowered Helleborine **10.**

45

9 Dune Helleborine
Epipactis dunensis

Other names Nil.

× ½, in fruit, Cumbria

Habitat and distribution

It is found on dune slacks only, though some may persist after such an area has been planted with alien conifers.

Distribution is very limited, though some colonies are large.

Flowering period

Mid June to early August, mostly in mid July, before the majority of Broad-leaved Helleborines **6.**

Field characters

Colour plate III(*d*).

Height 9–15 in (22–38 cm).

In general, the plant is like a small, dull, Broad-leaved Helleborine, but it has the following characters.

Few, small, stiff, yellow-green leaves, usually in two rows.

Flowers of a dingy yellow, rarely opening fully and often withering at an early stage.

The outer lip is pinkish with a pale green pointed tip (sometimes folded underneath).

Variation

Plants growing under trees are larger than average.

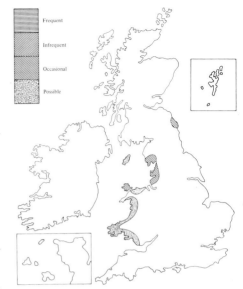

Frequent

Infrequent

Occasional

Possible

10 Green-flowered Helleborine
Epipactis phyllanthes

Other names Pendulous-flowered or Green Helleborine, *Epipactis viridiflora*. The species as now understood includes forms which were at one time considered distinct species: *E. vectensis* (Isle of Wight Helleborine), *E. pendula* and *E. cambrensis*.

× ⅔ Surrey

Habitat and distribution

It is usually found on calcareous or neutral soils, rarely on acid. The drainage seems immaterial: sites vary from dune slacks to roadside verges or river margins. Shade is usually moderate or light, and thick woods are not favoured. Accompanying trees may be beech, oak, birch, willow, hazel or introduced conifers; ivy is a common ground layer.

The few colonies are found mostly in southern England, least uncommonly in Hampshire and the Chilterns. It is probably still an overlooked species.

Flowering period

Early July to early September, mostly late July to early August.

Field characters

Colour plate III(*e*).
Height 4–24 in (10–60 cm).

The leaves are few (3–6), small, wavy edged and in two rows, the lowest only being usually rounded at the tip. They lack the rib-like veining common in other species of the genus. When on dunes, the leaves are a richer green than the Dune Helleborine.

The flowers usually hang almost vertically downwards; in some colonies they never open at all, in others they open partially.

The outer lip (when visible) is usually triangular, less pointed than in the Narrow-lipped Helleborine **8,** whitish or pale pink and not folded underneath.

In one extreme variation the lip is in one piece, lacking the cup-shaped inner section

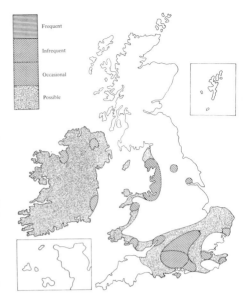

characteristic of all other flowers of the genus.

Variation

This is a self-fertile species, extremely variable between colonies, each of which is to some extent unique as regards flower structure.

11

Dark-red Helleborine
Epipactis atrorubens

Other names Small-flowered or Purple Helleborine,
E. rubiginiosa or *ovalis*.

× ½ Clare (M. C. F. Proctor, from a transparency)

Habitat and distribution

It is usually found on bare limestone cliffs or scree, sometimes in open ashwoods on steep limestone hillsides.

Distribution is wide but very local, chiefly in North Wales, the Pennines, the Lake District and western Ireland; many suitable sites are unoccupied.

Flowering period

Early June to late July; the great majority are out and over well before any Broad-leaved Helleborines **6** appear in the same area.

Field characters

Colour plate III(*f*).
Height 12–30 in (30–75 cm).

The leaves are dark green, few, in two rows, and usually (though not invariably) tinged with reddish on the underside.

The stem and ovary are downy (unlike the Broad-leaved) and the sepals and petals are blunter.

The flowers are usually smaller and a darker wine-red than any Broad-leaved, but they may occasionally be greenish.

The outer lip is broader, relative to its length, than the Broad-leaved, and has two rough bosses which are diagnostic.

Variation

Hybrids × Broad-leaved have been recorded.

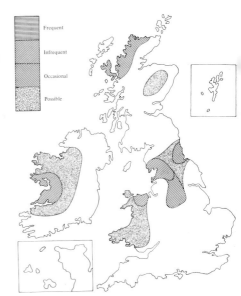

Frequent

Infrequent

Occasional

Possible

12

Ghost Orchid
Epipogium aphyllum

Other names Spurred Coralroot, Leafless Orchid, *Epipogium gmelini*.

× ⅔ Chilterns

Habitat and distribution

It is almost invariably on chalk or limestone, always in woods with heavy shade, on bare floors with a rich humus.

The species is an extreme rarity, with only two small fairly regular Chiltern beechwood colonies, though it has in the past been found elsewhere (on sandstone). It is probably an overlooked species.

Flowering period

It can flower any time from May to September, though late July and August seem to be the commonest. A wet period some weeks beforehand seems to be necessary for flower formation.

Field characters

Colour plate V(*a*).
Height 4–8 in (10–20 cm).

It is leafless with a yellow stem, though it may have one or two small brown bracts.

The flowers are few (usually single), relatively large and pendulous. Sepals and petals are pointed and yellowish, the lip is pink, purple veined and found at the top of the flower, unlike all other British and Irish orchids except for the totally dissimilar Bog Orchid **20** and Fen Orchid **21.**

The spur is blunt, uptilted and so fat that at first it may be difficult to recognise as a spur.

For the differences from the Coralroot Orchid **22,** see that species.

Variation

A constant species.

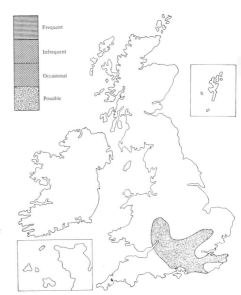

Frequent

Infrequent

Occasional

Possible

53

13 Autumn Lady's-tresses
Spiranthes spiralis

Other names Common Lady's-tresses.

× ⅘ Surrey

Habitat and distribution

It most often occurs on chalk or limestone downland in short turf, but has also been recorded from dunes and open sandy heaths, even lawns. Sites are open and almost invariably dry (unlike sites of all the other Lady's-tresses), though damp meadows have been recorded.

It is predominantly a southern plant, decreasing through undergrazing and agricultural destruction, but still capable of recolonising suitable sites at times. The number of flowers in a colony varies a good deal from year to year.

Flowering period

Early August to late September.

Field characters

Colour plate VI(*a*).

Height 3–8 in (7.5–20 cm).

The leaves lie flat on the ground in a rosette separate from the flowering stem, often not yet out at flowering time.

The slender spike has its small white flowers in a single row, usually arranged spirally around the stem. Clusters are not in-frequent in well-established colonies.

Next year's flowering stems arise from this year's non-flowering leaves.

Variation

The degree of spiral varies and may be absent altogether.

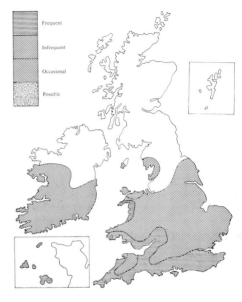

Frequent

Infrequent

Occasional

Possible

14 SUMMER LADY'S-TRESSES *Spiranthes aestivalis*

This is now extinct even in the Channel Islands, but could conceivably be found again in southern England. It is a marsh or bog plant only, with a taller, narrower flower spike (10–15 in, 25–38 cm) and, on the stem, slender erect leaves, which are out or even fading when in flower. On average, it flowers about three weeks earlier than the Autumn Lady's-tresses.

Irish Lady's-tresses
Spiranthes romanzoffiana

Other names American, Drooping or Cork Lady's-tresses, *Spiranthes gemmipara*. Northern Irish plants were at one time considered a separate species: Rydberg's Lady's-tresses, *Spiranthes stricta*.

× ¾, in bud, Antrim

Habitat and distribution

It is only found in wet places, watermeadows, lake margins and old peat workings, usually with a neutral water supply. It grows in short or medium length vegetation, usually in the open, sometimes between bushes; grazing is usually essential to its well-being.

It is found only in Ireland, a few places in west Scotland and one in Devonia but it may be expanding its range. The number in any colony varies much from year to year.

Flowering period

Late July to early September.

Field characters

Colour plate VI(c).
Height 4–12 in (10–30 cm).

The leaves are long and narrow, out at the same time and on the same stem as the flower.

The flowers are in three rows, giving a much fatter flower spike than other Lady's-tresses. Individual flowers are also larger than in other Lady's-tresses.

Variation

Northern Irish plants are leggier than southern ones, they have creamier-coloured flowers and their leaves are often rolled up at the edges, looking even narrower than usual. Non-Irish specimens are said to be intermediate in type.

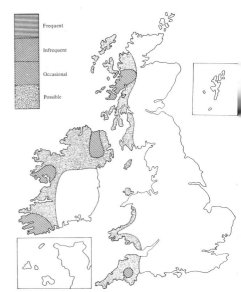

Frequent

Infrequent

Occasional

Possible

16 Twayblade
Listera ovata

Other names Common Twayblade.

× ⅔ Surrey

Habitat and distribution

Though most often on calcareous soils, it can occur almost anywhere except on very acid soils. It is equally frequent in open and shaded situations, which are usually well drained but some sites are very wet.

It is probably the commonest and most widely distributed of all our orchids, and colonies are sometimes very large.

Flowering period

Mid May to early August: there is a marked difference with latitude. Specimens in heavy shade are usually later than those in the open.

Field characters

Colour plate IV(*a*).
Height 6–24 in (15–60 cm).

The two large opposed elliptical leaves, starting from the stem well above ground level are distinctive. (A third leaf is very occasionally found, above the others.)

For distinctions from the Lesser Twayblade **17**, see that species.

The flowers themselves bear a first-glance resemblance to the Man Orchid **50** or the Frog Orchid **24**, but their leaves are entirely different.

Variation

Plants in heavy shade are taller and leggier than those in the open.

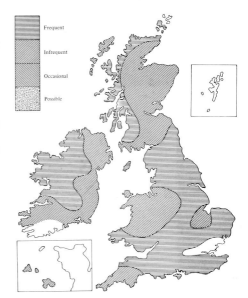

Frequent

Infrequent

Occasional

Possible

17

Lesser Twayblade
Listera cordata

Other names Nil.

× 2 Gwynedd

Habitat and distribution

The species requires acid soils and moist surroundings, almost invariably in hilly or mountainous areas. It occurs on well-drained moors or wet bogs (often facing north) with the plants more or less hidden among heather and/or sphagnum. It is perhaps commoner in open Scottish pine forests, occasionally in well-established plantations of alien conifers.

It is very local, even in Scotland, but is almost certainly an overlooked species.

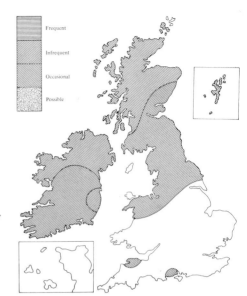

Flowering period

Late May to mid August.

Field characters

Colour plate IV(*b*).
Height $1\frac{1}{2}$–8 in (3–20 cm), often invisible from walking height.

It is much smaller than the average Twayblade, with leaves that are heart shaped, not elliptical.

The flowers usually have a reddish tinge and their lips are relatively longer, thinner and more deeply forked.

It can be an exceedingly difficult plant to see even when in flower, and non-flowering specimens (a high proportion in some colonies) may genuinely need a hands and knees search.

Variation

Pine-forest specimens are larger, easier to see and less reddish than the normal.

18

Bird's-nest Orchid
Neottia nidus-avis

Other names Nil.

× ½ Surrey

Habitat and distribution
Colonies are usually, though by no means invariably, on calcareous soil, always with a rich deep humus. The species is commonest in dark, bare-floored beechwoods, but is also found among oak, hazel and birch. Though usually in heavy shade, it does occur occasionally in open grass at wood edges, even on roadside banks.

It is commonest in the south. Numbers vary much from year to year.

Flowering period
Mid May to early July but mostly late May and early June.

Field characters
Colour plate V(*b*).
Height 6–18 in (15–45 cm).

The overall honey-brown colour is diagnostic. It could at first glance be confused with non-orchids such as broom-rapes, or yellow bird's-nest, but these lack the characteristic orchid structure, the bright yellow pollinia and the sickly fragrance.

Previous year's stems and seed heads may persist for many months, enabling colonies to be found even in the winter.

Variation
The flowers may rarely be pale yellow overall or even whitish.

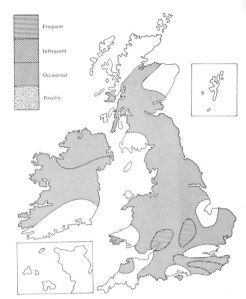

Frequent

Infrequent

Occasional

Possible

19

Creeping Lady's-tresses
Goodyera repens

Other names Nil.

× ¾ Norfolk

Habitat and distribution

This is a Scottish pine-forest species, usually in open stands, sometimes with birch. The plants themselves often grow in a layer of moss with thin heather, bilberries, etc. It occasionally grows in plain heather away from trees.

It also occurs as an accidentally introduced plant in pine plantations elsewhere, as far south as Norfolk, and this could perhaps happen almost anywhere in our islands. Colonies are often large.

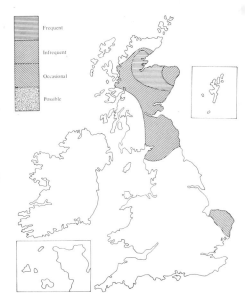

Frequent

Infrequent

Occasional

Possible

Flowering period

Early July to mid August.

Field characters

Colour plate VI(*d*).
Height 3–9 in (7.5–22 cm).

The leaves (on the stem and in separate rosettes) are short, broad, pointed and with discrete stalks (this last unlike any other British or Irish orchid) and usually a dark marbled green in colour.

The stem and flowers are notably downier than any other Lady's-tresses.

The flower head is usually shorter and broader than that of the Autumn **13** or Summer **14** Lady's-tresses, but nothing like as fat as the Irish **15.**

The flower lip is narrow and spout shaped.

Variation

Apparently a constant species.

20

Bog Orchid
Hammarbya paludosa

Other names *Malaxis paludosa.*

× 1½ New Forest

Habitat and distribution

It frequents only wet bogs with moderately acid drainage water, almost invariably growing in sphagnum cushions. It seems to prefer 'flows' or the edges of pools, where the moss never dries out even in a hot summer and the water is always moving slowly.

It is least rare in the north, but always very local, and is probably an overlooked species. In southern England, Hampshire and Dorset are its chief areas. Appearance may be sporadic, with widely varying size of colony.

Flowering period

Early July to early September, mostly mid July to mid August.

Field characters

Colour plate V(c).
Height 1½–5 in (3–12.5 cm), often impossible to see from walking height.

The flowers are tiny, yellow-green and with the lip at the top of the flower, unlike all other species except the totally dissimilar Ghost Orchid **12** and the Fen Orchid **21**.

It has no spur.

Variation

A constant species.

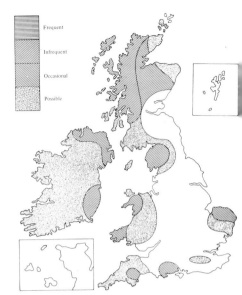

Frequent

Infrequent

Occasional

Possible

21

Fen Orchid
Liparis loeselii

Other names Nil.

Broad-leaved ssp, × ¾ Glamorgan

Habitat and distribution

The typical subspecies, *Liparis l. loeselii*, occurs in wet fens with moderate cover, usually inland from the tall reed belt: an alkaline water supply is essential.

This occurs now only in East Anglia and is fast becoming very rare because of the lowering of the water table at most sites.

The ssp *ovata*, Broad-leaved Fen Orchid, occurs on dune slacks in South Wales and Devonia and appears to be increasing its range.

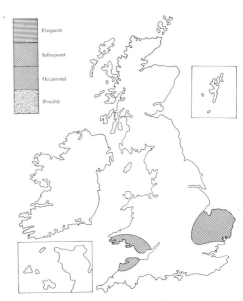

Flowering period

Early June to early July.

Field characters

Colour plate V(*d*).
Height 2–10 in (5–25 cm).

It is a smallish, dingy, yellow-green plant, easily overlooked, particularly in the generally taller vegetation of the typical ssp's habitat.

The yellow-green leaves (usually two) have a peculiar greasy texture.

The head is a loose spike of tiny green-yellow flowers, many of the floral parts looking like whiskers.

The lip is usually (but not always) at the top of the flower, like the Bog Orchid **20,** but it has a totally different habitat.

It has a prominent spur.

Variation

The dune slack ssp is shorter, with broader blunter leaves, which are egg shaped instead of elliptical.

22

Coralroot Orchid
Corallorhiza trifida

Other names Common Coralroot, *C. innata.*

× ¾ Fife (J. Caldwell)

Habitat and distribution

It requires damp situations with a rich humus. The commonest site is boggy pinewood, sometimes with birch, but it also occurs in willow or alder scrub and (commonly in places) on dune slacks in the open.

It is very local in Scotland, and rare in the north of England.

Being inconspicuous, and often growing in situations little visited by botanists, it could be an overlooked species.

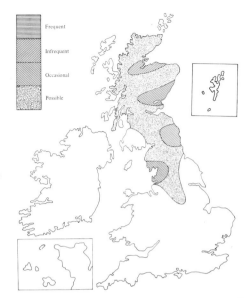

Flowering period

Mid May to early August, mostly early June to early July.

Field characters

Colour plate V(e).
Height 3–9 in (7.5–22 cm).

It is a brownish-yellow plant with a green tinge in places, without leaves, though it may occasionally have the odd bract.

The flowers are small (sometimes very small), with down-curved sepals and a roughly three-lobed, red-spotted white lip.

The lip is the 'right way up', unlike the Ghost Orchid **12,** from which it has a quite different known distribution.

Variation

It is a constant species, except in the size of the actual flower which can vary considerably.

23

Musk Orchid
Herminium monorchis

Other names Nil.

× ⅘ Surrey

Habitat and distribution

Colonies are invariably on chalk or limestone, in well-drained situations, always in the open and on short turf. The species is particularly fond of old chalk workings now grassed over.

Colonies are infrequent but may be very large. Numbers in each vary much from year to year.

Flowering period

Early June to mid July.

Field characters

Colour plate V(*f*).
Height 2–9 in (5–22 cm); single individual plants are easily over-looked from walking height, but groups can be conspicuous.

The habitat rules out con-fusion with most of the other species which have tiny yellow-green flowers. Individual flowers are smaller than those of the Frog Orchid **24,** and the lip has a different, barbed-arrow, shape. The flowers smell of honey, not musk.

Variation

A constant species.

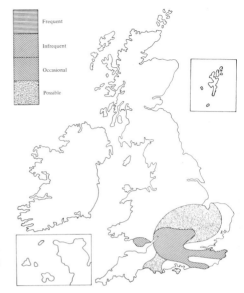

Frequent

Infrequent

Occasional

Possible

24

Frog Orchid

Coeloglossum viride

Other names *Habenaria viride.*

× ⁴⁄₅ Antrim

Habitat and distribution

The type of soil is immaterial (provided it is not too acid or too rich) but good drainage and an open situation are essential. It usually grows among short grass on downs or poor meadows, often on north-facing slopes. Dune slacks and Hebridean 'machair' are also favoured.

Numbers in most colonies vary greatly from year to year. It is a widespread species but always very local, being commonest in the north of Scotland and Ireland.

Flowering period

Early June to early August.

Individual flowers may be long lasting.

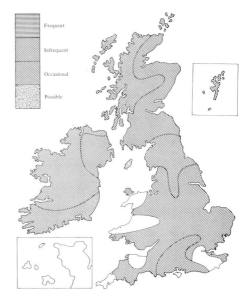

Frequent

Infrequent

Occasional

Possible

Field characters

Colour plate IV(c).

Height 2–12 in (5–30 cm); it may be difficult to see from walking height.

It can be distinguished as follows from other dry-site species with small greenish flowers.

From the Twayblade **16** by having broad, blunt leaves of 'normal' orchid type.

From the Man Orchid **50** by the lack of 'arms' on the scarcely-divided lip and the presence of a spur, albeit short and blunt.

From the Musk Orchid **23** and Broad-leaved Fen Orchid **21** by the quite different shape of the flowers.

Variation

There appear to be two forms: one very short and with a reddish tinge (commonest in the south), the other relatively tall and green (commonest in the north).

Hybrids have been recorded with several species, the results being intermediate in form and often bizarre in appearance: that × Fragrant Orchid is named × *Gymnaglossum jacksoni* (Quick) Rolfe.

Fragrant Orchid
Gymnadenia conopsea

Other names Scented or Gnat Orchid, *Habenaria conopsea* or *G. conopea*

× ½ Surrey

Habitat and distribution

The typical ssp is a plant of calcareous soils in warm dry situations in lowland England. A variant form is common on hill pastures in North Britain and Ireland.

It is widely distributed and colonies may be large.

Flowering period

Early June (typical ssp) to early August (Marsh ssp).

Field characters

Colour plate VII(a).
Height 4–18 in (10–45 cm): Marsh Fragrant up to 30 in (75 cm).

The strongly keeled leaves are in rows 180° apart.

The pink unmarked flowers and very long spur distinguish it from all but the Pyramidal Orchid **51**, from which it may be differentiated by the longer, roughly cylindrical flower spike and (usually) paler colour and less deeply lobed lip. It also lacks the Pyramidal's distinctive lip ridges.

Variation

The flower colour can vary from white to bright magenta.

Hybrids have been recorded × Frog Orchid, Small-white Orchid, Pyramidal Orchid and various Spotted- and Marsh-orchids, but they are uncommon.

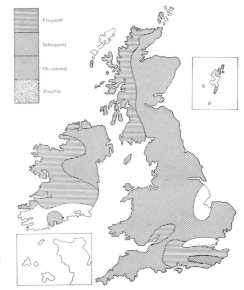

Frequent

Infrequent

Occasional

Possible

The MARSH FRAGRANT ORCHID, *Gymnadenia conopsea densiflora*, is a generally larger and sturdier plant with relatively broad leaves; it grows in calcareous or neutral marshes or on wet hillsides. The flowers are a deeper pink, with a relatively broader lip, and the flowering date is two to three weeks later on average. In some areas, for example East Anglia, this is the only ssp present.

The Marsh ssp smells of cloves, whereas the typical ssp usually has a sickly-sweet scent; the hill-pasture form (which may be an undescribed third ssp) smells of cloves also.

26 SHORT-SPURRED FRAGRANT ORCHID *Gymnadenia odoratissima*

This was recorded once in Durham in 1912 and might conceivably recur from continental seed on chalk or limestone. It has narrower leaves than the Fragrant Orchid, smaller flowers and a spur only half as long, i.e. the same length as the ovary.

77

Small-white Orchid
Pseudorchis albida

Other names Small-white Mountain, White Fragrant, or White Frog Orchid, *Habenaria, Gymnadenia* or *Leuchorchis albida.*

× ⁴⁄₅ Yorkshire

Habitat and distribution

The species is largely indifferent to soil type which, however, must be of poor quality and never strongly acid. It occurs on hills and mountains only, usually above 500 feet (165 m), in rough pastureland, upland hay meadows or, sometimes, in short heather on mountains. Though other orchid species are usually present, it does sometimes grow on its own.

It is uncommon anywhere, possibly an overlooked species.

Flowering period

Mid May to mid July, mostly in June and earliest in the south.

Individual flowers are very short lived, almost invariably setting seed.

Field characters

Colour plate VI(*e*).
Height 4–12 in (10–30 cm).

The small size and narrow spike of tiny white flowers preclude confusion with most other species.

Flowering date alone differentiates it from the Lady's-tresses (quite apart from their spiral flower arrangement, their leaves and habitats).

The three roughly equal lip lobes and absence of a hood distinguish it from the Dense-flowered Orchid **30,** though the flowers do often face one way, inviting initial confusion.

The very short blunt spur distinguishes it from small, white-coloured specimens of the Fragrant Orchid **25** or the Irish Common Spotted-orchid **43.**

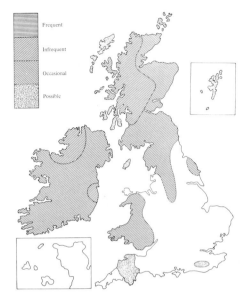

Frequent

Infrequent

Occasional

Possible

Variation

A constant species.

Hybrids × Fragrant Orchid have been recorded. The species often grow together.

28

Greater Butterfly-orchid
Platanthera chlorantha

Other names *Habenaria chlorantha* or *virescens*.

Woodland form, × ⅔ Surrey

Habitat and distribution

The species can be found in a wide variety of situations, wet or dry, open or shaded, though there is, perhaps, some preference for alkaline soils. It occurs in woods, scrub, downland, hill pastures and occasionally peatbogs provided these are not too acid, that is without sphagnum.

Though it is widely distributed it is a scarce species even in southern England and many suitable sites are unoccupied. It may grow in company with the Lesser Butterfly-orchid **29,** but it is generally commoner in the south than in the north.

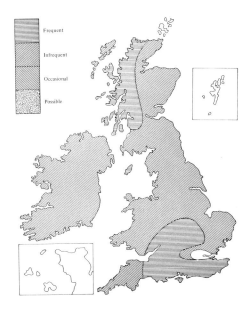

Frequent

Infrequent

Occasional

Possible

Flowering period

Early June to late July.

Field characters

Colour plate IV(*e*).
Height 8–24 in (20–60 cm).

It is unmistakable except for resemblance to the Lesser Butterfly **29,** from which it can be distinguished by the following characters.

Slightly larger, on average, with a sturdier build.

A wider flower spike with the flowers on longer stalks.

Flowers more often greenish in colour.

Pollen masses relatively far apart and divergent, with a wider mouth to the spur (2 mm or more).

Variation

Woodland plants are taller, slimmer and more greenish than those growing on moorland.

Hybrids × Lesser Butterfly (*Platanthera × hybrida,* Bruegger) have been recorded but are rare, as also are hybrids × Common and Heath Spotted-orchids.

29

Lesser Butterfly-orchid
Platanthera bifolia

Other names *Habenaria bifolia.*

Moorland form, × ½ Londonderry

Habitat and distribution

Details are exactly the same as for the Greater Butterfly **28** except that it is much more tolerant of acid soils, and it is commoner in the north than in the south, though still a scarce species.

Flowering period

Late May to late July.

Field characters

Colour plate IV(*f*).
Height 6–15 in (15–37 cm).

For distinctions from the Greater Butterfly **28,** see that species.

The pollen masses in this species are parallel and close together, and the mouth of the spur is narrower (1 mm or less).

Variation

There is much the same difference between woodland and moorland forms as in the Greater Butterfly. The moorland form of this species has shorter, egg-shaped leaves.

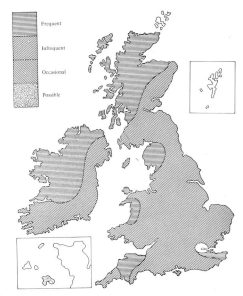

Frequent

Infrequent

Occasional

Possible

30

Dense-flowered Orchid
Neotinea intacta

Other names Close-flowered or Irish Orchid, *Habenaria
intacta*.

× ⅔ The Burren (A. H. Aston, from a transparency)

Habitat and distribution

A mild moist climate is required. It is usually on limestone, with thin plant cover, but occasionally on stabilised dunes or soil just inland with some overblown sand.

It is rare. Apart from one colony in the Isle of Man, it is only known from the west of Ireland (the Burren and a few nearby districts). It might possibly turn up in Northern Ireland, the Inner Hebrides or southwest England.

Flowering period

Early May to early June. (In its areas, it is one of the very earliest species.)

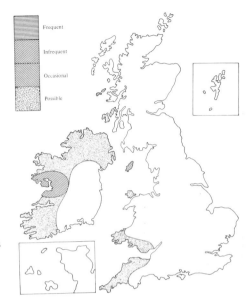

Field characters

Colour plate VI(*f*).
Height 4–12 in (10–30 cm).

It has a short dense spike of flowers (usually all facing one way) of a white or pale-pink colour.

For features distinguishing it from the Small-white Orchid **27,** see that species.

The lip shape which is long, notched at the tip and with very small side lobes, rules out confusion with the Irish Common Spotted-orchid **43,** as does its *orchis*-like hood.

It flowers long before any of the Lady's-tresses (see these species for other differences).

Variation

Some of the pink-flowered specimens (only) have spotted leaves.

31 Bee Orchid
Ophrys apifera

Other names Nil.

× ½ Surrey

86

Habitat and distribution

It is commonest on chalk or limestone, but also occurs on sand, clay, dune slacks and in disused gravel pits. Open sites, short grass and good drainage seem essential, though it is occasionally found in woods (especially in the Chilterns).

The species is generally scarce, though well-established colonies may at times be very large; numbers in colonies vary much from year to year. It can colonise waste ground better than most orchids, but usually only for a short period.

Flowering period

Late May to early July (mostly during June); woodland and northerly plants are the latest.

Field characters

Colour plate XII(*a*).
Height 4–20 in (10.5–50 cm).

The general resemblance of the lip to a furry insect distinguishes it from all but the Spider-orchids **32** and **33.**

The side lobes separated from the main lip, and having the apical point tucked underneath, distinguish it from either Spider-orchid. For further distinctions, see those species.

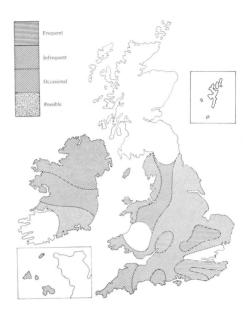

Frequent

Infrequent

Occasional

Possible

Variation

In these islands the species is usually self-pollinated, so colonies tend to be alike but to vary from other colonies.

Lip marking is particularly variable. Semi-albinos have been recorded. f. *trollii* ('Wasp Orchid') has the apical point dagger-shaped and not folded under. This often has a variegated lip pattern and has most often been found in the Cotswolds: it has been suggested as a good ssp.

Hybrids × Late and Early Spider-orchid have been recorded (*Ophrys* × *albertiana*, Camus, and *Ophrys* × *pseudoapifera*, Camus, respectively).

32

Late Spider-orchid
Ophrys fuciflora

Other names *Ophrys arachnites.*

× ¾ Kent

Habitat and distribution

It is only found on chalk down-land with short grass. Through destruction of habitats and undergrazing in the last half-century, a heavy decline has taken place.

Only a very few small colonies remain, in east Kent, but it could conceivably be found else-where in southeast England, from windborne continental seed.

Flowering period

Late May to early July, on average, a week or so earlier than the Bee Orchid.

Field characters

Colour plate XII(*b*).
Height 4–15 in (10–45 cm).

It is usually shorter in the stem and less obvious than the Bee Orchid **31,** from which it is distinguished by having a larger squarer, flatter and furrier lip which is more russet coloured. Also its apical point turns upwards and its side lobes are integral with the main lip.

It is distinguished from the Early Spider-orchid **33** by its later flowering date, furrier and more russet-coloured lip (with a different marking pattern) and by having pink sepals.

It has much smaller, downier petals than either the Bee or Early Spider-orchids, and they are triangular in shape.

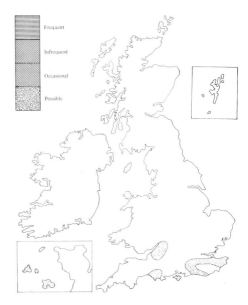

Variation

The lip shape and pattern vary a good deal and the sepals are sometimes white instead of pink, but never green or yellow.

Hybrids × Bee, and Early Spider (*Ophrys × obscura,* G. Beck), have been recorded.

33

Early Spider-orchid
Ophrys sphegodes

Other names Spider Orchid, *Ophrys aranifera*.

× ⁴⁄₅ Kent

Habitat and distribution

It is almost always found on chalk or limestone in short grass, very rarely on sand dunes. Many colonies are close to the sea, though it does occur inland.

It is rare and very local in south and southeast England, many sites having been destroyed in recent years or too little grazed, but some colonies in the extreme south are still very large.

Flowering period

Early April to late May. (With the Early-purple, it is our earliest Orchid species.) Colonies vary a good deal in date.

Field characters

Colour plate XII(*d*).
Height 2–9 in (5–23 cm).

It has a diagnostic blue H or Pi (π) mark on the lip. For other features distinguishing it from Bee **31** and Late Spider-orchids **32,** see those species.

Variation

The lip pattern varies much and the marking colour fades with age. Some lips are self-coloured.

Hybrids are unlikely here because of the earlier flowering date of this species, but they have been recorded × Late Spider, Bee, and Fly Orchids. (For scientific names see those species.)

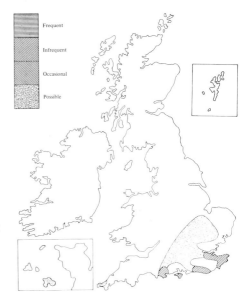

Frequent

Infrequent

Occasional

Possible

34

Fly Orchid
Ophrys insectifera

Other names *Ophrys muscifera.*

× ½ Surrey

Habitat and distribution

It occurs almost always on chalk or limestone, usually at wood edges or in clearings, often in quite heavy shade. It can also be found in scrub, uncommonly in the open. Sites are usually well drained, but (rarely) can be marshy, especially in Ireland.

It is a widespread but scarce and always very local plant: many apparently suitable sites are unoccupied. Despite its striking appearance close to, it is easily overlooked.

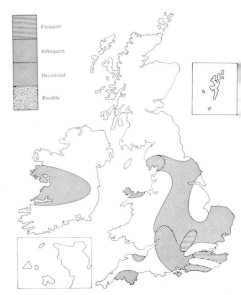

Frequent

Infrequent

Occasional

Possible

Flowering period

Late April to late June.

Field characters

Colour plate XII(*e*).
Height 6–24 in (15–60 cm).

The lip shape, pattern and colouring are diagnostic.

Variation

Plants in heavy shade are leggier than those in more open sites. Partial albinos have been recorded, but the shape of the lip should still be unmistakable.

Hybrids × Early Spider-orchid have been recorded, but are very rare (*Ophrys × hybrida*, Pokorny).

35

Lizard Orchid
Himantoglossum hircinum

Other names *Orchis hircinum* or *hircina*.

×⅓ Kent

Habitat and distribution

Invariably it occurs on calcareous soils—chalk, limestone or stabilised dunes—often with long grass or marram, sometimes with bushes too.

A very few apparently permanent colonies exist in east and southeast England; elsewhere it has been found in small numbers for a few years only, as far north as Yorkshire.

The population is probably reinforced at times by continental seed, and it may be increasing its range.

Flowering period

Late June to mid July.

Field characters

Colour plate VIII(*f*).
Height 9–30 in (23–75 cm).

The combination of usually large size, stout build, grey-green colour and long lips in the rough shape of lizard tails is quite unmistakable. When flowers are not quite open, the lip is coiled up like a watch spring. In bloom, the flowers have a smell resembling (to some people) that of a goat.

The leaves are usually withered by flowering time.

Variation

The colour of the lip varies somewhat and darkens with age.

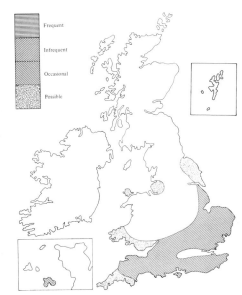

Frequent

Infrequent

Occasional

Possible

36

Lady Orchid
Orchis purpurea

Other names Brown-winged Orchid, *Orchis fusca*.

× ½ Kent

Habitat and distribution

It invariably occurs on chalk, usually in scrub or woodland, rarely on open downland.

The species is widespread in Kent (though local) and a very few colonies may still exist in Surrey and Sussex. Colonies are gradually decreasing in number, though some are still large. It might occur elsewhere in England from windborne seed. Single specimens have been found in the Chilterns and in Herefordshire in recent years.

Flowering period

Late April to early June.

Field characters

Colour plate VIII(*b*).
Height 8–36 in (20–90 cm).

The large size, stately appearance and the dark chocolate-coloured or purple-flecked hoods are a diagnostic combination. It is perhaps the most striking in appearance of all our orchids.

For other features distinguishing it from the Monkey **38** and Military **37** Orchids, see those species.

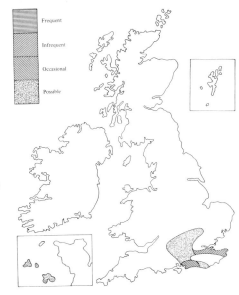

Frequent

Infrequent

Occasional

Possible

Variation

Specimens from southwest of the River Stour are said to be generally shorter than those from northeast of the river, with denser flower spikes and more spots on the lip. Lip details are very variable.

Occasional specimens (especially when going over) have shrunken 'bloomers' and resemble the Military Orchid **37** but for the colour of the hood.

Albinos have been recorded, also forms with three lips per flower.

37 Military Orchid
Orchis militaris

Other names Soldier Orchid.

× ⅔ Chilterns

Habitat and distribution

It occurs invariably on chalk, in not too well-drained situations, preferring clearings or glades in woods, or grassland with light scrub cover.

The species rapidly decreased in the last century and for a while in the 1920s and 30s was thought to be extinct. It is now known from three sites in the Chilterns and one in East Anglia. Overlooked sites might exist, and colonies could be founded elsewhere in southeast England from windborne continental seed.

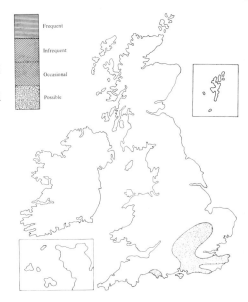

Frequent

Infrequent

Occasional

Possible

Flowering period

Mid May to late June.

Field characters

Colour plate VIII(*a*).
Height 8–18 in (20–48 cm).

It can be distinguished from the Lady Orchid **36** by its generally rather smaller size, narrower lip (with much narrower crimson 'legs' widening at the extremities) and the absence of brownish-purple on the hood, which has long, pointed, ashen coloured sepals.

Compared with the Monkey Orchid **38,** it is usually larger, has a looser flower spike and has thicker 'legs', widened at the ends, rather than parallel, narrow and kinked.

Variation

East Anglian specimens are looser flowered than Chiltern ones, with paler, narrower 'legs'.

Hybrids × Monkey Orchid have been recorded on the Continent (*Orchis × beyrichi,* A. Kerner) but are most unlikely here.

38

Monkey Orchid
Orchis simia

Other names Nil.

× ½ Kent

Habitat and distribution

It occurs on chalk or limestone, in well-drained situations, usually in the open, though it can persist in intrusive scrub (even when this has become a tall scrubby copse); stabilised dunes are a possibility.

The species rapidly decreased in the last century in the Chilterns (which was then its only area) but was discovered in Kent in the 1950s. There are now two known Chiltern colonies, and three in Kent. Occasional specimens have occurred elsewhere in southern areas (presumably from wind-borne continental seed), and it has recently been reported from Yorkshire. The numbers in the colonies vary a good deal from year to year.

Flowering period

Mid May to mid June.

Field characters

Colour plate VIII(c).
Height 6–12 in (15–30 cm).

The brightly coloured puppet-like lip is unmistakable except for resemblance to the Military Orchid **37,** from which it is distinguished by the following features.

It is usually smaller with a shorter, denser flower spike.

The 'figure' has thinner parallel-sided 'legs', usually kinked.

The flowers usually open from the top of the spike downwards.

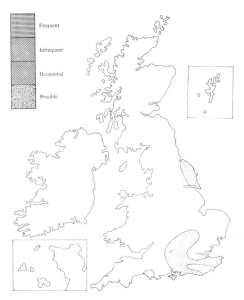

Frequent

Infrequent

Occasional

Possible

Variation

Chiltern specimens are generally shorter and more brightly coloured. Some Kentish specimens (but not all) open in the conventional orchid way—from the bottom of the spike upwards.

39

Burnt Orchid
Orchis ustulata

Other names Dwarf or Burnt-tip Orchid.

× ⅘ Sussex

Habitat and distribution

The species usually occurs on chalk or limestone, sometimes on gravel or sand. It requires short grass and good drainage.

It is now rare and always very local; colonies are decreasing, through agricultural destruction of sites and undergrazing, though some large ones remain. The numbers in any colony vary much from year to year.

Flowering period

Mid May to the end of July, varying by colony; most are early.

Field characters

Colour plate VIII(*d*).
Height 1½–8 in (3.5–20 cm).

Superficially it resembles a miniature Lady Orchid **36** but the lip shape is different. The 'burnt' appearance of the flower spike is due to the tight packing of the individual flowers' chocolate hoods.

Variation

The size of the plants varies between colonies and with the year; some are very small and inconspicuous indeed.

The chocolate hood colour gets paler as the flower goes over; in bad seasons (wet or very dry), flowers may wither without opening properly at all.

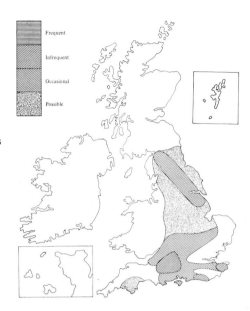

Frequent

Infrequent

Occasional

Possible

40 Green-winged Orchid
Orchis morio

Other names Green-veined Orchid. It has also some local English names.

× ¼ Kent

Habitat and distribution

It occurs now usually on calcareous soils, sometimes on clay or gravel. It is never found in true woodland but usually in short grass on hillsides (preferably not too well drained), often with cowslips.

Formerly common on old pastures, it is now a scarce species, always local, with many suitable sites unoccupied. Some colonies, however, are still large. It is decreasing, perhaps more than any other species, through agricultural destruction of habitats.

Flowering period

Early May to late June, according to latitude, most being in late May.

Field characters

Colour plate VIII(*e*).
Height 3–12 in (7.5–30 cm), often an inconspicuous plant despite its rich colour.

The general appearance is similar to the Early-purple Orchid **42** except for the following features.

It is generally smaller and often much smaller.

It never has spotted leaves (the Early-purple often does).

The sepals have prominent dark veins which are always obvious.

It has a much tighter and less spreading hood.

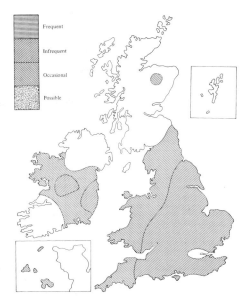

Frequent

Infrequent

Occasional

Possible

Variation

The flower's ground colour can vary from white, through rose-pink to a dark bluish-purple, which is much the commonest.

Hybrids × Early-purple have been recorded (*Orchis × morioides*, Brand).

41 Loose-flowered Orchid
Orchis laxiflora

Other names Jersey Orchid.

106

×⅔ Channel Islands (E. Ferbrache, from a transparency)

Habitat and distribution

It grows in damp grassy places and marshes, never in woods.

Known only from the Channel Islands, it could conceivably occur elsewhere in southern England from windborne continental seed.

Flowering period

Early May to mid June.

Field characters

Colour plate VII(*e*).
Height 6–18 in (15–45 cm).

The species is similar to the Early-purple Orchid **42** except that it has the following distinguishing characters:

A looser flower spike which may be obvious from quite a distance.

Leaves narrow, erect and never spotted, while the Early-purple's often have spots.

Bracts with three veins, Early-purples usually having one only.

A lip with two lobes only, instead of three.

A spur shorter than the ovary, instead of longer.

Variation

Hybrids × Green-winged Orchid have been recorded in the Channel Islands (*Orchis × alata,* Fleury).

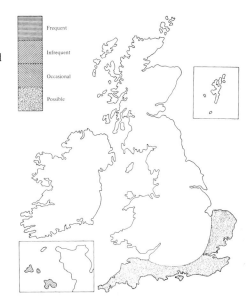

Frequent

Infrequent

Occasional

Possible

42 Early-purple Orchid
Orchis mascula

Other names It has numerous English country names.

× ½ Surrey

Habitat and distribution

It is most often found on calcareous soils, but it will also grow on neutral or even (rarely) on acid ones. In the south, it is commonest in coppiced woods, often with bluebells and/or dog's mercury. It also occurs on open downland, road verges, cliffs, etc.

Colonies are widespread and often large, the numbers in each varying a good deal from year to year. In woodland, there is often a marked increase after the making of clearings or coppicing.

Flowering period

Early April to late June, according to latitude and year.

Field characters

Colour plate VII(*d*).
Height 3–18 in (7.5–45 cm).

The purple colour and broad three-lobed lip are obvious features.

It could only be mistaken for the Green-winged **40** or Loose-flowered **41** Orchids; for the differences, see those species.

Variation

Some lips are plain purple, others have a pale centre with a few dark spots. Pale pink or even white specimens are found sometimes.

Specimens in the open are smaller and stockier than woodland ones.

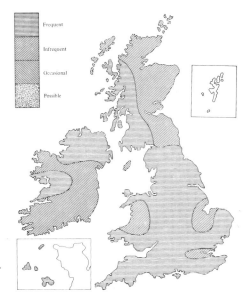

Frequent

Infrequent

Occasional

Possible

Common Spotted-orchid
Dactylorhiza fuchsii

Other names Woodland Spotted Orchid *Orchis* or
Dactylorchis fuchsii, or *O. maculata* var. *meyeri*. Both
subspecies have at times been treated as full species.

×⅔ Surrey

Habitat and distribution

It occurs commonly on cal-careous soils, also on non-acidic clays or loams. The drainage is immaterial: dry downland and marshes with standing water are equally suitable. It is usually in the open or in light scrub, sometimes in open woods and on woodland roadside verges. It is commonest in the south and colonies are often very large.

Flowering period

Late May to late July (latest in woods and in the north).

Field characters

Colour plates IX(*a*), (*c*) and (*e*). Lip shape diagram p. 117. Height 4–30 in (10–75 cm). The species could only be con-fused with the Heath Spotted **44** but the Common Spotted shows the following distinctions.

The lowest leaf short, broad and rounded at the tip but not always visible.

Leaf spots, when present, which are solid and transversely barred.

Narrow lip lobes, roughly equal in size (or the centre one longest).

Lip markings in the form of dashes or loops rather than dots.

A thicker, more tapering spur.

Variation

The woodland form is taller, leafier and with a looser flower spike. The Hebridean Common Spotted-orchid, *D. fuchsii hebridensis*, occurs on dunes and

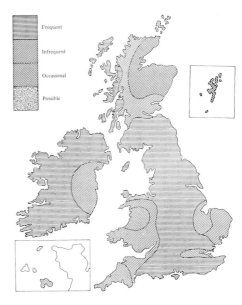

Frequent

Infrequent

Occasional

Possible

'machair' in the Hebrides, West Ireland and Devonia. It is small, very stocky, and a deeper pink than the type, with a very broad lip and a prominent central lip lobe. The Irish Common Spotted-orchid, *D. fuchsii okellyi*, occurs in Ireland and a few places in west Scotland. It is a slender plant with few narrow unspotted leaves and a narrow spike of small white or only faintly marked flowers. Lip sides are more rounded than in *f. fuchsii*; individual plants of this description are sometimes found elsewhere, however, and identification by colony is par-ticularly important with this ssp.

44 Heath Spotted-orchid
Dactylorhiza maculata ericetorum

Other names Moorland Spotted Orchid, *Orchis* or
Dactylorchis maculata, O. ericetorum or *elodes.*

× ⅔ Surrey

Habitat and distribution

The soil is usually acid, sometimes neutral, rarely alkaline. Drainage is immaterial: sites may be on sphagnum bogs or dry moors.

It is commonest in the north and west.

Flowering period

Late May to late July, according to latitude and altitude.

Field characters

Colour plates IX(*b*), (*d*) and (*f*). Lip-shape diagram p. 117. Height 4–30 in (10–75 cm).

The following characters distinguish it from the Common Spotted **43.**

All leaves are pointed and usually narrow.

Leaf spots (relatively infrequent) are usually small and round.

The centre lobe of the lip is smaller than the side ones, which are usually very broad and rounded.

Lip markings are in the form of dots or light dashes rather than heavy dashes or loops.

The spur is more pointed and only half to two-thirds as thick.

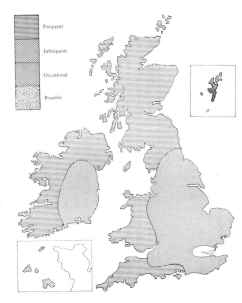

Frequent

Infrequent

Occasional

Possible

Variation

The ssp Rhum Heath Spotted-orchid, *Dactylorhiza maculata rhoumensis*, is known from Rhum and probably some other Inner Hebridean islands, growing on 'machair' and adjacent areas with some wind-blown sand on them. The lip shape is generally the same as the Heath Spotted (though some specimens may have a well-developed centre lip lobe), the leaves are always identical, but the lip markings are like the Common Spotted, consisting of heavy dashes or even loops. The colour, however, is never the dark pink found in most Hebridean Common Spotted-orchids.

113

45 Early Marsh-orchid
Dactylorhiza incarnata

Other names Marsh or Crimson Marsh Orchid, *Orchis* or *Dactylorchis incarnata*, *O. strictifolia* or *latifolia*.

Purple ssp, × ⅔ Surrey

Habitat and distribution
The species occurs in a wide range of wet or damp habitats, nearly always on calcareous or neutral soils; when in bogs, the drainage water is usually lime-rich.

Flowering period
Late May to mid July, according to latitude and subspecies.

Field characters
Colour plate X. Lip-shape diagram p. 117.
Height 6–20 in (15–50 cm).

The stem is usually fat and hollow, the leaves erect, tapering, yellow-green and hooded at the tip, i.e. slightly cupped, like a bluebell's.

Individual flowers are small compared with other Marsh-orchids, with lips of rounded diamond shape but looking very narrow because the sides are sharply folded back (as are the sepals).

Lip markings are in the form of curved dashes or double loops.

The spur is short, distinctly curved and tapering.

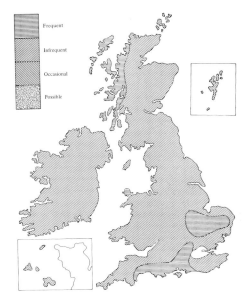

Frequent

Infrequent

Occasional

Possible

Variation
Because of their number, the subspecies are dealt with separately on p. 116. Individual flowers in any colony may vary from white to dark purple, but the majority will be of the colour appropriate to the subspecies; however, colonies of mixed subspecies can occur.

A few widespread colonies have large flowers and lip markings in the form of small dots only, other features being like the type; this has been ascribed at times to a ssp *gemmana* (Pugsl.) Sell, but here it is considered only a form.

Typical subspecies

Dactylorhiza incarnata incarnata
All the comments on p. 115 apply. The flower colour is usually a diagnostic pale flesh-pink. It is scarce, though widely distributed.

Purple Early Marsh-orchid

Dactylorhiza incarnata pulchella
The flowers are a bright reddish-purple, otherwise it is like the type. It is widely distributed, usually, but not exclusively, on relatively acid bogs (often with sphagnum). Bracts may be purple, as with the Northern Marsh-orchid. It is local and uncommon.

Dune Early Marsh-orchid

Dactylorhiza incarnata coccinea
The flowers are a distinctive deep brick-red colour, otherwise it is like the type. It grows in dune slacks (most dune systems other than in eastern England have this plant) and occasionally in similar habitats, for example sand-covered hollows on shallow clay cliffs in East Anglia. It is local and uncommon.

Flecked Early Marsh-orchid

Dactylorhiza incarnata cruenta
The flowers are similar to the Purple subspecies but the leaves are heavily marked on both sides with reddish-brown spots (sometimes the bracts and stem are too). The lips are less folded and appear broader than the Purple ssp. It occurs only in western Ireland, around calcareous loughs and has often been quoted as a full species: Flecked or Connaught Marsh-orchid, *Dactylorhiza cruenta*. On the other hand, it seems to occur usually with other ssp, and eventually it may turn out to be a mere form, analogous to f. *pardalina* in the Southern Marsh-orchid. It is rare.

Fen Early Marsh-orchid

Dactylorhiza incarnata ochroleuca
This has flowers of a yellowish-white, usually unmarked and with a brighter yellow patch near the base of the lip; a shadowy lip pattern (of the usual type for the species) may be acceptable. The lip is distinctly three-lobed, though still folded back slightly at the sides: a case has been made for full specific status. Herbaria have specimens from places as remote as Orkney, but it is more likely that the ssp only occurs now in the inland fens of East Anglia where it is very rare.

Lip shapes

Figure 4.1 shows an average selection of Spotted- and Marsh-orchid lip shapes. Variation outside these examples is considerable, and they should be taken as showing trends rather than limits.

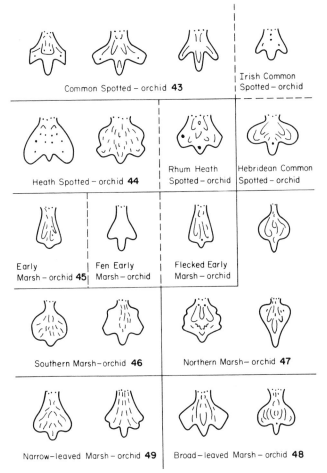

Figure 4.1 Spotted and Marsh-orchid lip shapes.

117

46 Southern Marsh-orchid
Dactylorhiza praetermissa

Other names Common or Purple Marsh-orchid, *Orchis* or *Dactylorchis praetermissa*.

× ⅔ Glamorgan

Habitat and distribution

The species favours calcareous or neutral marshes and water-meadows, also dune slacks and occasionally dry places such as chalk downland (ephemerally and in small numbers). Overall, it is now scarce.

Flowering period

Early June to mid July, about two weeks later on average than the Early Marsh-orchid **45** where they occur together.

Field characters

Colour plate XI(*a*). Lip-shape diagram p. 117.
Height 6–28 in (15–70 cm).

It is generally larger than the Early Marsh, with a thinner, less hollow stem, and broader, darker, lightly hooded leaves (though exceptions occur).

Bracts are usually green (unlike the Northern Marsh **47**) but may be purplish.

The lip is roundish, flat or slightly dished, not folded back.

The colour is a pinkish-purple, often lighter in the centre and almost always paler than any Northern Marsh.

Lip markings usually consist of small dots, not long dashes or loops, mostly in the central area.

The spur is thick, slightly curved and tapering.

Note that none of these characteristics is absolutely diagnostic—colonies vary a lot and it is the combination which counts.

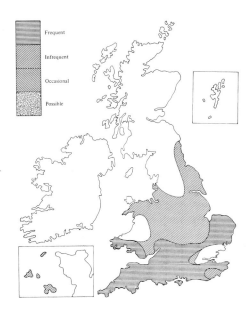

Variation

Chalk downland specimens are often very small.

Flower colour varies from pale pink to deep magenta, seemingly by area. f. *junialis* has small solid spots on the leaves; f. *pardalina* ('Leopard Marsh-orchid') has heavy hollow-ringed leaf spots and often has heavier lip markings than usual: either form may be a constituent proportion of any colony.

47 Northern Marsh-orchid
Dactylorhiza purpurella

Other names Dwarf Purple Orchid or Dwarf Marsh-orchid, *Orchis* or *Dactylorchis purpurella*.

× ⅔ Londonderry

Habitat and distribution

Though most often on calcareous or neutral soils, it can also grow well on moderately acid ones. It occurs in a wide variety of wet habitats such as marshes, watermeadows, peatbogs, dune slacks.

The distribution is mostly north and west, and complements that of the Southern Marsh. Though very numerous in places, particularly in Ireland, its general status is scarce.

Flowering period

Mid June to late July.

Field characters

Colour plate XI(*c*). Lip-shape diagram p. 117.
Height 4–10 in (10–25 cm), occasionally to 18 in (45 cm).

Though often small, it is usually similar in size to other

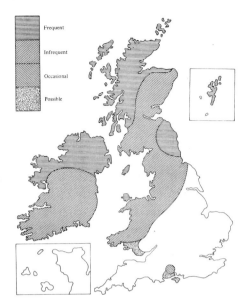

Frequent
Infrequent
Occasional
Possible

tapering than that of the Early Marsh **45**.

Variation

Lip colour and markings are fairly constant, but other characters vary a good deal.

The leaves are fairly broad, spreading or erect, slightly hooded at the tip; their colour is sometimes darker than the Early Marsh **45** but not always. Leaf spots, if present, are small, solid and mostly near the tip.

The bracts, and sometimes the stem, are stained with purple.

The flower spike is dense, and usually flat topped, with flowers of a rich reddish-purple which are usually darker and more bluish than any Southern Marsh **46**.

The lip is broad, flat, three-lobed or kite shaped, marked with heavy dashes and loops.

The spur is thick, usually less

48 Broad-leaved Marsh-orchid
Dactylorhiza majalis

Other names *Dactylorchis* or *Dactylorhiza occidentalis*, *Dactylorhiza* or *Orchis kerryensis* or *O. latifolia*. The BSBI-preferred name is Irish Marsh-orchid (they do not mention the Welsh subspecies).

Irish ssp, × ½ Galway (M. C. F. Proctor, from a transparency)

Habitat and distribution

It can occur on any sort of soil, from acid bogs with Heath Spotted-orchids to the calcareous Burren lakesides, in boggy places or wet meadows, rarely on dune slacks.

Small numbers can persist for a while after the planting of alien conifers.

Flowering period

In Ireland it flowers from mid May to mid June, the earliest of all Marsh-orchids there, while in Wales flowering is from mid June to mid July.

Field characters

Colour plate XI(*d*). Lip-shape diagram p. 117.

Height 4–15 in (10–45 cm).

The leaves are broad (sometimes extremely so) and dark green, spreading, not sharply pointed and not hooded. They are almost always well marked with large rounded spots or blotches.

The flowers are large and reddish-purple, often dark (lacking the extreme depth of colour common in the Northern Marsh **47**) but occasionally very pale.

The lip is flat or with slightly folded side lobes, broader than long, often angular in outline and notched, with the centre lobe projecting beyond the sides. Markings are dashes and loops, usually less heavy than in the Northern Marsh.

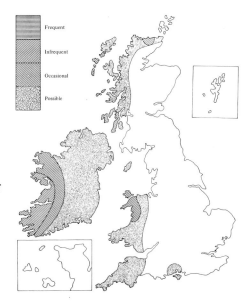

Frequent

Infrequent

Occasional

Possible

Variation

The Irish Broad-leaved Marsh-orchid, *Dactylorhiza majalis occidentalis*, occurs rarely in western Ireland and west Scotland.

The Welsh Broad-leaved Marsh-orchid, *Dactylorhiza majalis cambrensis*, is the ssp found very rarely in north and west Wales. It has longer leaves and a straighter spur.

Narrow-leaved Marsh-orchid
Dactylorhiza traunsteineri

Other names Wicklow or Pugsley's Marsh-orchid,
Orchis or *Dactylorchis traunsteineri*, *angustifolia*,
traunsteineroides or *majalis traunsteineroides*.

× ⅓ Oxon

Habitat and distribution

It habitually grows in fen-type marshes on calcareous soils or with alkaline drainage water, usually in standing water, sometimes with reeds. It has also been recorded in wet calcareous meadows.

Known localities are few and widely scattered but it may well be an overlooked plant.

Flowering period

Early May to late June, mostly in early June.

Field characters

Colour plate XI(*b*).
Lip-shape diagram p. 117.
Height 6–18 in (15–45 cm).

The leaves are few, long and narrow, usually erect; the tips are pointed but not (or only slightly) hooded. The leaf spots (rarely present) are small and usually transversely barred, near the tip of the leaf.

The flower spike is slender, often one-sided and with fewer flowers than others of the genus. It also often appears much looser—an unexpectedly obvious feature at times.

The flowers are a reddish-purple (never as deep as most Northern Marsh-orchids **47**) with loop, line or, most often, dash markings on the lip.

The lip is three lobed, with the side lobes usually well rounded and a longish pointed or triangular centre lobe.

The spur is fat, straight or down-curved and cylindrical, almost as long as the ovary.

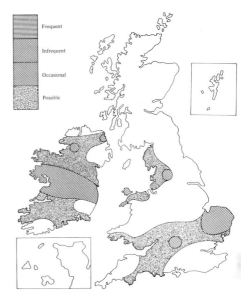

Frequent

Infrequent

Occasional

Possible

Variation

All characters are variable between colonies (particularly the overall size).

50 Man Orchid
Aceras anthropophorum

Other names Green Man Orchid, *Orchis anthropophorum*.

× ⅔ Surrey

Habitat and distribution

It occurs invariably on well-drained calcareous soils, in the open or in thin scrub, rarely in woods. It is often (but not always) on the lower slopes of hillsides.

Though the species is rare, colonies are frequent in Kent and Surrey. It may be extending its range, where suitable sites remain.

Flowering period

Mid May to early July, mostly during June.

Field characters

Colour plate IV(*d*).
Height 4–20 in (10–50 cm), depending largely on the length of the ambient grass.

The combination of yellowish-green flower colour and puppet-like flowers is almost conclusive.

The presence of 'arms' and better-developed 'legs' distinguish it from the Twayblade **16,** apart from that species' leaf arrangement.

For differences from the Frog Orchid **24,** see that species.

It has no spur, which is diagnostic.

Variation

Many specimens have a certain amount of reddish-brown in the flower coloration.

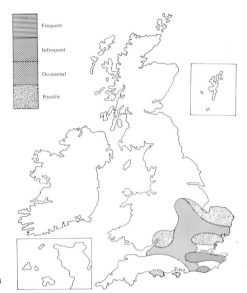

Frequent
Infrequent
Occasional
Possible

51 Pyramidal Orchid
Anacamptis pyramidalis

Other names *Orchis pyramidalis.*

× ⅘ Devon

Habitat and distribution

It only grows on calcareous soils with good drainage, mainly chalk or limestone hill slopes, or sand dunes, but it can persist in scrub and, rarely, in woods.

It is common in the south and colonies may be very large.

Flowering period

Early June to late August, mostly late June to early August.

Field characters

Colour plate VII(*c*).
Height 6–18 in (15–45 cm).

The combination of un-marked pink flowers, narrow unspotted leaves and long spur distinguish it from all but the Fragrant Orchid **25** but it may be separated from that species by the following features.

A dense round or conical flower spike and usually a deeper colour.

Much narrower, divergent lip lobes.

Two upright longitudinal ridges on the lip, which are diagnostic.

Variation

The colour may vary from the usual purplish-pink through salmon to white.

Hybrids × Fragrant Orchid (× *Gymnacamptis anacamptis* (Wilm.) A. & G.) and × Common Spotted-orchid have been recorded.

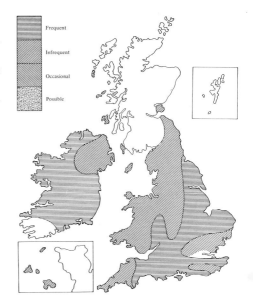

Frequent

Infrequent

Occasional

Possible

5 Colour plates

Plate I Putative hybrid: Common × Heath Spotted-orchid (*Dactylorhiza × transiens*).

Plate II (*a*) Lady's-slipper **1**, Pennines (A. Butcher). (*b*) White Helleborine **2**, Surrey. (*c*) Narrow-leaved Helleborine **3**, Hampshire. (*d*) Red Helleborine **4**, Cotswolds. (*e*) Marsh Helleborine **5**, Glamorgan.

Plate III (*a*) Broad-leaved Helleborine **6**, Surrey. (*b*) Violet Helleborine **7**, Surrey. (*c*) Narrow-lipped Helleborine **8**, Surrey. (*d*) Dune Helleborine **9**, Cumbria. (*e*) Green-flowered Helleborine **10**, Surrey. (*f*) Dark-red Helleborine **11**, Cumbria.

Plate IV (*a*) Twayblade **16**, Surrey. (*b*) Lesser Twayblade **17**, Gwynedd. (*c*) Frog Orchid **24**, Devon (M. C. F. Proctor). (*d*) Man Orchid **50**, Surrey. (*e*) Greater Butterfly-orchid **28**, Surrey. (*f*) Lesser Butterfly-orchid **29**, Kent.

Plate V (*a*) Ghost Orchid **12**, Chilterns. (*b*) Bird's-nest Orchid **18**, Surrey. (*c*) Bog Orchid **20**, New Forest. (*d*) Fen Orchid **21**, East Anglia. (*e*) Coralroot Orchid **22**, Perthshire. (*f*) Musk Orchard **23**, Surrey.

Plate VI (*a*) Autumn Lady's-tresses **13**, Surrey. (*b*) Summer Lady's-tresses **14**, Brittany (F. Rose). (*c*) Irish Lady's-tresses **15**, Antrim. (*d*) Creeping Lady's-tresses **19**, East Anglia. (*e*) Small-white Orchid **27**, Inner Hebrides (P. Corkhill). (*f*) Dense-flowered Orchid **30**, The Burren (A. H. Aston).

Plate VII (*a*) Fragrant Orchid **25**, Surrey. (*b*) Marsh Fragrant Orchid, Norfolk. (*c*) Pyramidal Orchid **51**, Surrey. (*d*) Early-purple Orchid **42**, Surrey. (*e*) Loose-flowered Orchid **41**, Channel Islands (J. D. Bichard).

Plate VIII (*a*) Military Orchid **37**, Chilterns. (*b*) Lady Orchid **36**, Kent. (*c*) Monkey Orchid **38**, Chilterns. (*d*) Burnt Orchid **39**, Sussex. (*e*) Green-winged Orchid **40**, Buckinghamshire. (*f*) Lizard Orchid **35**, Kent.

Plate IX (*a*) Common Spotted-orchid **43**, Surrey. (*b*) Heath Spotted-orchid **44**, Surrey. (*c*) Common Spotted-orchid, Irish ssp, Londonderry. (*d*) Heath Spotted-orchid, Ross. (*e*) Common Spotted-orchid, Hebridean ssp, Outer Hebrides (G. Rodway). (*f*) Heath Spotted-orchid, Rhum ssp, Rhum.

Plate X (*a*) Early Marsh-orchid **45**, typical ssp, Norfolk. (*b*) Early Marsh-orchid *f. gemmana*, Hants. (S. R. Davey). (*c*) Early Marsh-orchid, Purple ssp, Surrey. (*d*) Early Marsh-orchid, Dune ssp, Londonderry. (*e*) Early Marsh-orchid, Fen ssp, Suffolk.

Plate XI (*a*) Southern Marsh-orchid **46**, Glamorgan. (*b*) Narrow-leaved Marsh-orchid **49**, south-central England. (*c*) Northern Marsh-orchid **47**, Gwynedd. (*d*) Broad-leaved Marsh-orchid **48**, Welsh ssp, Gwynedd. (*e*) Northern Marsh-orchid, Antrim. (*f*) Broad-leaved Marsh-orchid, Welsh ssp, Gwynedd.

Plate XII (*a*) Bee Orchid **31**, Surrey. (*b*) Late Spider-orchid **32**, Kent. (*c*) 'Wasp' Orchid, Cotswolds (J. G. Keylock). (*d*) Early Spider-orchid **33**, Sussex. (*e*) Fly Orchid **34**, Surrey.

Plate
I

Plate
II

a

b

c

d

e

Plate
III

a

b

c

d

e

f

Plate
IV

a

b

c

d

e

f

Plate
V

a
b
c
d
e
f

Plate
VI

a

b

c

d

e

f

Plate
VII

a

b

c

d

e

Plate
VIII

a

b

c

d

e

f

Plate
IX

a

b

c

d

e

f

Plate
X

a

b

c

d

e

Plate
XI

a

b

c

d

e

f

Plate
XII

a

b

c

d

e

6 Hunting for orchids

There is no great problem, technical or ethical, about looking for species whose status is scarce or common. The distribution maps show the general areas of occurrence and relative abundance, and the habitat and distribution sections of the species pages show what sort of ground within these areas is most likely to produce the required plants. A check against a fairly large-scale map (1:50 000 or 1 inch to 1 mile minimum) will indicate likely spots, and a personal reconnaissance, perhaps by car, will show up both advantageous and adverse features not marked on the map. From there it is just a question of looking around these suitable sites. It may take time, if luck is against you, but success is reasonably sure in the end.

A useful feature of the orchid scene is that ground suitable for one species is often suitable for others too. Many, perhaps most, of our orchids grow in mixed colonies, so the presence of a common species when searching for a scarcer one is a hopeful sign.

Even when looking for the more obvious plants (Helleborines, for example) there is a temptation to walk too fast, in order to cover as much ground as possible. This should be resisted; one's reception of visual data falls off roughly as the square of one's speed. Anyone seeing a Fly Orchid colony for the first time can verify this. The first flower noticed is most striking and beautiful, almost impossible to miss, one would think, but on walking around the site really slowly, the number of flowers to be found will be quite astonishing. A good basic walking rate is one pace per second: when 'hot on the scent' it should be slower still.

Several small species are described in the species pages as difficult to see from walking height but few genuinely need a hands and knees search at the beginning, for some relatively large individual specimen will catch one's eye and then the slow, stooping (or hands and knees) search can begin in earnest.

Incidentally, it is surprising how quickly the eyes become adjusted to the search; after finding one flower of an inconspicuous type (and subconsciously memorising its appearance) others appear thick and fast even in places previously scrutinised. It is a good idea to study the colour flower-head plates before starting such a search.

One point that must not be forgotten in assessing search areas is the length of the orchid life cycle. From four to fifteen years have been quoted for our species' seed-to-flower periods, and there is field evidence for a period of seven years for the Monkey Orchid.

These, of course, are in favourable conditions. Considering the seasons when no seed is set, when it rots on the flower because of wet weather, or fails to be captured by the symbiotic fungus needed for germination, it is clear that the foundation of a colony (which may need several generations to reach any size) may be a long-term business. On downland, for instance, there are usually noticeably fewer orchids in areas that were under the plough till the 1920s than in adjacent areas of a hundred or more years' undisturbance: this applies to numbers not only of individuals but of species. As a generalisation, the more antique the site in its present form, the greater the number of orchids to be found there.

Woodland species

Woodland species of orchid will only be found in any quantity where woods have been managed (preferably for centuries) on the old system of individual fellings, or very small block fellings, which allows the plants to spread back quickly from the intact areas. The modern system of clear-felling whole woods, or very large blocks, is highly destructive to orchids even in the cases when native hardwoods are replanted, and that ubiquitous pollutant the alien conifer utterly destroys most orchid colonies.

Grassland species

Reverting to grassland species, many become choked if surrounding vegetation grows unchecked for more than a few years. Traditionally, grassland orchid sites depend on grazing, preferably by sheep (whose feet do less physical damage to the surface in wet weather) but also very successfully by cattle in some places.

Grazing can be overdone and the optimum balance is a fine one, but established orchids are a long-lived, hardy lot, and a regime of, say, two years' overgrazing, one year's undergrazing and one year's optimum grazing will not affect the population seriously, though there will only be a good show of flowers in the optimum year.

In Ireland, Scotland, Wales and northern England, the number of old grazed meadows and hillsides is still reasonably satisfactory; the chief threat to orchids there is the increasing use of fertilisers, as few species will tolerate a rich soil.

On the chalk downlands and limestone wolds of southern England, however, grazing has declined catastrophically in the last forty years, and many old orchid sites have been overwhelmed by scrub, when not ploughed up for arable use. This is not the place to discuss the various grazing substitutes used by conservation authorities, but there is one type of site which still has short grass even when ungrazed, where the soil is so very thin that rank vegetation simply cannot grow and scrub cannot invade.

Such sites do rarely occur naturally, on very steep scarps that were once sea or river cliffs, for example, but the great majority are man-made. Combining this with the comments made earlier about the need for long periods of undisturbance, one is led directly to the types of site which in practice prove the most productive: old grassed-over chalkpits, the banks of ancient track-ways and the ramparts of old hillforts. If looking for chalk downland orchids these are the first places to search. As time goes by, more recent works of man will become equally good. For example some railway embankments are now over a hundred years old and 1938-vintage by-pass road cuttings can already show modest orchid colonies; eventually we may reach a situation where motorway banks become the chief reservoirs of our downland species.

Marsh and fen species
The state of our orchids in marsh and fen-type habitats in southern England is parlous; for example, there are perhaps only two or three colonies of the Early Marsh-orchid in the whole county of Sussex, despite the numerous stream and river valleys and 'levels'. Rivers, streams and drainage dykes are now 'cleaned' (dug out and the banks denuded of vegetation) at intervals far less than orchids can tolerate. With the quicker water flow given by this clearance, marshes and 'levels' are steadily becoming drier and many which were wet grazing even thirty years ago are now growing arable crops. In East Anglia (except on public-amenity Broads and those Reserves where water levels are artificially maintained) the lowering of the water table has meant that many traditional fens can now be walked on dryshod, and the growth of scrub is reaching explosive proportions. Plants such as the Fen Orchid and the Fen Early Marsh-orchid have become very rare.

In small compensation, man-made marshes (the edges of gravel pits and brickyards) do provide some suitable habitats, but only on a transient basis because they are eventually taken over by scrub, and there is a regrettable tendency for planning authorities to require such places to be returned to agriculture when working has ceased.

Rare species
For rare and very rare species, the chances of a reader being able to find known colonies on the basis of this book have been discussed on p. 4.

The author does not agree with the proposition that it is immoral even to try to do so, still less with the suggestion that all information on rarities should be suppressed lest someone among those whose interest is aroused might turn out to be a villain.

If the discoverer of a new rarity site prefers to keep his find secret, he should take care that his conservation arrangements are watertight. Private landowners can die, or change their policies overnight because of financial pressures. Public bodies are even less reliable; a certain colony of the Welsh Broad-leaved Marsh-orchid was quite wantonly 95 per cent destroyed by the planting of alien conifers, although the public landowning body was fully aware of its rarity and importance; a colony of the Green-flowered Helleborine in southeast England is cut down three years out of four because the highways authority is so inefficient that it cannot honour its own agreement not to mow that roadside verge.

As a general proposition, the greater the number of responsible people who know of a rarity site, the safer it is from accidental or wilful destruction. For a quarter of a century the locality of one of our extreme rarity sites was known to a mere handful of people. In that time, a road could have been driven through the site, the farmer could have planted it with pit-props or put a byre unit on it and, most likely, that handful of people would not have found out in time to do anything preventive.

But for the very rare species this brings a most vexed problem: the damage caused by even well-meaning visitors in large numbers. That such damage can occur at times is unquestionable, chiefly through trampling of non-flowering plants, but it must be balanced against the proposition (not universally accepted) that the maximum practicable public access ought, as of right, to be allowed. If a plant cannot be seen by anyone except the Reserve Management Committee, it might just as well be extinct from the point of view of most people.

Obviously some restrictions on visits are inevitable at extreme-rarity sites. When there is a risk of the trowel-carrying lunatic fringe appearing (Military Orchids have been seen at the Chelsea Flower Show) then an absolute prohibition may be justified. At the time of writing, one such site has an electrified fence; another has a Rolls-Royce type of iron fence, and a few selected members of the public are admitted on two occasions during the flowering season as long as they do not stray from the duckboards provided. At one (wardened but free-access) site, however, between one and three hundred visitors appear annually, with or without cameras, and there has been no record of any damage to the plants in consequence. Protection and a liberal visiting policy are not necessarily mutually exclusive.

One gets the impression that the ascribing of population reductions to over-visiting is sometimes a convenient excuse for the conservation authority's having done nothing positive about conservation, even scrub clearance in one instance. A certain, and admirable, authority does allow a reasonable number of genuinely interested visitors (though certainly not all and sundry) on a freely-wandering basis to one of its rarity sites. This attitude is made possible because the authority has adopted a highly successful programme of individual protection of the plants from rabbits and of manual pollination of the flowers (this species rarely sets seed naturally). The consequent increase in the population has meant not only that occasional accidental trampling by visitors can be tolerated but even that daughter colonies can be founded from its seed in other localities. This is first-class positive conservation, which ought to be substituted for mere negative restriction elsewhere, whatever the thoughts of those old-fashioned people who would, it seems, rather see a species extinct than helped by such 'artificial' methods.

However, the author would urge that if rarity sites are discovered or learned of, this knowledge should not be abused; when a site has been visited once, a long period should be left before a revisit, in order to minimise accidental damage, as well as giving other plantsmen a chance to enjoy the sight of one of our beautiful rarities without incurring restrictions on access. The greatest care should be taken in passing on localities one has discovered and, if told of a site in confidence, that confidence must be honoured one hundred per cent, however close the friend who asks for details.

Further identification

Finally, some advice on what to do if a found plant remains a mystery even after careful study of plates and species pages. Do not take a physical specimen unless this is specifically requested by some authority, but instead take a photograph or, if possible, a series of photographs in colour at various reproduction ratios, and show it in the first instance to an experienced botanist or plantsman from the local Naturalists' Trust or Natural History Society. If satisfactory identification does not result, consider carefully how important the matter is. If it is just a question of to which common species the specimen belongs, the matter should be left there, but if it seems really important, indicating possibly a new site for one of the rarer Marsh-orchids or re-discovery of a lost species in that area, then one would be justified in going to a final court of appeal—one of the National Botanic Gardens or National Museums, or, if one is a member of the BSBI, one of its appointed Referees. These will not appreciate having their time wasted by trivialities, but will genuinely welcome inquiries of real or potential importance. (Return postage for anything sent for examination is a proper, if unusual, courtesy.)

If one of these experts asks for a physical specimen it can be provided with a clear conscience since sophisticated identification techniques (cytological examination of pollen and chromosome counts) do require actual material to work on. They will not ask for more than is necessary, and will not repeat the awful example of the Short-spurred Fragrant Orchid, whose only known UK specimen has reposed between blotting paper at Kew ever since its discovery.

7 Notes on the photography of orchids

Collecting orchid specimens for one's own amusement is indefensible, and even for scientific study it should only be carried out in the last resort (see p. 135). As for educational purposes, it is strange that some schoolteachers are still found among the orchid-pickers; nature-study teaching ought to involve a proper sense of conservation. The Conservation of Wild Creatures and Wild Plants Act, 1975, is a good UK beginning to protection by law.

In situ photography is for most people the only practicable way of recording their finds or of obtaining trophies. Incidentally, trophy hunting in itself is often considered undesirable, an attitude which seems to deny one of man's fundamental traits. Provided it is carried out with the strictest care not to damage accidentally the plants which the trophy hunter is equally anxious to preserve, photography is a perfectly acceptable activity, even by people who are not qualified botanists.

However, photographers have a poor reputation in the botanical world, exaggeratedly so, in the author's view, and quite avoidably so if only photographers would always follow the precepts of the Association of Natural History Photographic Societies' *Nature Photographers' Code of Practice* (published on its behalf by the Royal Society for the Protection of Birds). Suitable extracts are reprinted (with the Association Executive's permission) at the end of this chapter.

This is not the place to discuss the advantages and short-comings of all available pieces of photographic gear, nor to try to teach basic photography. What follows is a set of conclusions from the author's experience, making the assumption that the reader already has some general knowledge of photography.

Equipment

While there are points in favour of other types of camera and sizes of film, the best all-round camera for orchid photography is unquestionably the 35 mm single-lens reflex (SLR). With considerable ease of use, it can provide black and white prints of good quality up to a size of 380 × 305 mm (15 × 12 in), and colour transparencies good enough for lectures and normal page-size book or article illustrations.

Colour negative material is of small value, since the definition is poorer than in any black and white or reversal-colour material. Colour prints, too, have vastly less realism and colour-depth than transparencies and are much more prone to fading.

Among black and white films (and surprisingly few people seem to take black and white photographs of orchids) those of about

400 ASA are quite adequate for 250 × 200 mm (10 × 8 in) prints; they give good gradation, and have the advantages of enabling high shutter speeds to be used in good lighting (thus reducing the likelihood of camera shake or subject movement in wind) and enabling poorly lit subjects to be taken without recourse to flash. Slower film (125 ASA, or even 25–50 ASA at times) will give better quality provided one's optics and processing techniques are equal to it.

Among colour-reversal films, the same arguments apply in favour of high-speed material, but here the grain is often rather excessive, and the colour-saturation notably less than in slower materials. With the slower films (25–64 ASA), the chief consideration is usually the quality of the colour which is a matter of highly individual opinion since two people's ideals are rarely identical. Even objectively, 25 ASA is somewhat slow for many subjects, and films of 50/64 ASA are the most generally popular.

The actual model of 35 mm SLR matters little. A fully automatic diaphragm (FAD) is almost indispensable for hand-held work and a high flash-synchronisation speed for the shutter is a considerable advantage. An easy-loading device is a help, as is the capacity for fitting a magnifier or right-angle finder to the eyepiece. It is strongly advisable that the focusing screen should be capable of focusing subjects accurately at its corners or edges, even if not as quickly or conveniently as by whatever aid (split-prism or microprism) is fitted at the screen centre.

In the author's view, through-the-lens (TTL) metering is an expensive and unnecessary luxury. A separate incident-light meter of good quality is both cheaper and more consistently accurate.

Only in unusual cases, for example when outside one of the wired-in rarity sites (p. 134), will a long-focus lens (135 or 200 mm) be needed. Incidentally, wire mesh can safely be ignored from a photographic point of view if the lens can be kept close to it; this will then be so out of focus that it will not register, apart perhaps from reducing the overall contrast slightly.

A standard (50 or 55 mm) focal-length lens is generally adequate, though a semi-wide-angle lens (of 35 mm focal length) will give better perspective separation between the plant and its background. Most such lenses will not focus closer than 380–460 mm (15–18 in), too far for flower-head closeups or for whole-plant shots of the smaller species. Auxiliary close-focusing aids must be used: extension tubes (which need an exposure increase to make up for the increased distance of the lens from the film plane) or supplementary lenses (which ought to be of cemented-achromat construction if of greater power than +2 dioptres). A better solution is to use one of the so-called 'macro' lenses (of which most manufacturers list examples); they enable focusing to be carried out down to reproduction ratios of 1:2 (adequate for flower-head shots of most species) without auxiliary aids; some go down to 1:1, but few of these retain the FAD facility.

Most macro lenses need additional exposure at the closer ranges, as with standard lenses plus extension tubes; a very few, however, compensate for it by opening up the iris automatically as the lens is racked forward. For cameras with the common Pentax/ Praktica/Edixa body thread, there is at the time of writing one lens of 35 mm focal length, f2.8, focusing to 1:2.2, with auto and compensating iris mechanism—the GDR Zeiss Flektogon: it really is almost the ideal orchid-photography lens, though curiously enough it is usually only advertised as a plain semi-wide-angle.

Artificial lighting is often necessary, either in situations where the ambient light is inadequate, or to reduce the risks of camera shake and subject movement in better lighting. Only the use of single small electronic-flash sets need be considered here. The manufacturers' guide numbers are rarely accurate in outdoor closeup situations, and precalibration of such sets is essential; the use of a flash-meter (borrowed, for preference, as they are expensive to buy) is strongly desirable for this calibration process. Flash heads should be used with 30–45° separation from the camera (to give shadows in natural-looking positions) and should *never* be used at or below camera level. A reflector made from white card, held near the plant, will help soften the otherwise hard shadows from the single light source.

Ring flash is a great help for 'diagrammatic'-type shadowless closeups, giving good modelling and illumination of cavities in the subject. Many of the colour illustrations in this book were taken this way.

Camera technique

Wrong camera position is one of the two commonest causes of poor orchid photographs. The major point here is the camera–subject distance; one *must* fill the frame with the intended picture (bearing in mind that the 'picture' may include some of the subject's surroundings). The other is one of viewpoint-height; the best, for whole-plant shots, is only slightly above the centre of the plant, and for flower-head shots the camera should be exactly opposite the centre of the subject.

The second common fault is wrong choice of aperture, which should give a depth of field sufficient (and only sufficient) to cover the main subject, whether whole plant or flower head. Many whole plants of medium sized orchids can be covered quite adequately at f6.3–8; to use f16 in such circumstances will make the background oversharp and destroy the necessary impression of separation. For closeups of flower heads, however, the depth of the subject can only be covered at f16 (or, better, f22 if the lens will stop down that far) and an exposure at f8, say, will render much important detail out of focus and blurred.

Of course, circumstances often require that photographs are taken in difficult conditions or with apparatus that is not entirely suitable. The highest quality is not always attained but it is always worth attempting since, through trying, one's standard steadily improves.

Extracts from the Nature Photographers' Code of Practice

'The welfare of the subject is more important than the photograph' is a rule which must be closely observed at all times.

This is not to say that photography should not be undertaken because of slight risk to a common species, but the amount of risk acceptable decreases with the scarceness of the species and the photographer should always do his utmost to minimise it. Risk in this context means risk of physical damage, consequential predation or lessened reproductive success.

The photographer should be familiar with the natural history of his subject; the rarer the species the greater his knowledge ought to be. He should also be sufficiently familiar with other natural history specialities to be able to avoid damaging their interests accidentally. Photography of scarce animals and plants by people who know nothing of the risks involved is to be deplored.

For many subjects, 'gardening' (that is, interference with surrounding vegetation) is necessary. This should be to the minimum extent, not exposing the subjects to predators, people or adverse weather conditions. It should be carried out by tying back rather than cutting off and the vegetation should be restored to as natural a condition as possible after each photographic session.

Trampling of habitats can cause serious damage in vulnerable areas, especially marshes. It is essential that preparations to photograph one specimen of a rarity do not involve treading on other specimens, including non-flowering ones. Tracks to and from a rarity should be devious and inconspicuous and should be restored to naturalness afterwards.

Plant photographers should be familiar with the Botanical Society of the British Isles' *Code of Conduct* and *List of Rare Plants*. While these allow the picking of moderate rarities, photographers should take a more restrictive view. No rarity should be picked (still less dug up) for studio photography or to facilitate the *in situ* photography of another specimen. Nor should parts of one be removed to facilitate the photography of another part.

If the photograph of a rarity is to be published or exhibited, care should be taken that the site location is not accidentally given away.

It is important for the good name of nature photography that its practitioners observe normal social courtesies. Permission should be obtained before operations on land to which there is not customary free access, and other naturalists should not be incommoded. Work at sites and colonies which are the subjects of special study should be coordinated with the people concerned.

Photographs of cultivated or otherwise controlled specimens may be of genuine value but should never be passed off as wild. Users of such photographs (for exhibition or publication) should always be informed, however unlikely it may seem that they care.

Recommended reading

Wild Orchids of Britain, V. S. Summerhayes, Collins, New Naturalist series, 2nd edition, London (1968). Though now slightly out of date in a few ways, this is an absolute *must* for anyone seeking depth in his knowledge of our orchids.

An Excursion Flora of the British Isles, Clapham, Tutin and Warburg, Cambridge University Press, 2nd edition, Cambridge (1968). This is a shorter and slightly more up-to-date version of the standard British Flora, though it is now distinctly out-of-date in some orchid respects. Plants and their parts are fully and technically described, and the tyro plantsman may find the jargon well-nigh impenetrable.

Europaeische und Mediterrane Orchideen, H. Sundermann, Bruecke Verlag Kurt Schmersow, 2nd edition, Hildesheim (1975). Perhaps the best book dealing with European orchids outside these islands, it is very well illustrated but unfortunately the text is in German. There is no book in English on this topic which can be wholly recommended, though *Orchids of Europe*, A. Duperrex, Blandford (1961), can be useful at times.

The Pollination of Plants, M. C. F. Proctor and P. Yeo, Collins, New Naturalist series, London (1973). The subject is as stated, but much space is devoted to orchids and the illustrations are excellent.

Natural History Photography, D. M. T. Ettlinger *et al.*, Academic Press, London (1974). The chapter on plant photography is by M. C. F. Proctor and is considerably more detailed than the treatment here.

Finding Wild Flowers, R. S. R. Fitter, Collins, London (1971). While the book deals with all our wild flowers, it gives some very useful localities for particular types of habitat in each county or small group of counties. For the commoner species of orchid, sites can readily be deduced from some of these, but the author is properly careful not to mention any of the major rarity sites.